2/00

Versailles,
the American Story

This work has been published with the support of Veuve Clicquot Ponsardin
in memory of La Grande Dame de la Champagne

ISBN 2-909838-44-7

©1999, Alain de Gourcuff Éditeur, 18, rue d'Aumale, Paris IXe

Versailles, the American Story

Pascale Richard

Translated from the French by Barbara Mellor

Editorial director: Emmanuel Ducamp

ALAIN de GOURCUFF ÉDITEUR

This letter encapsulates
the generosity of
American patronage
of Versailles and
its special place in the
history of Franco-
American friendship.

Monsieur Raymond Poincaré,
de l'Académie Française
Président du Conseil des Ministres,
Paris, France.

May, 3, 1924.

My Dear Mr. President:

Returning to France last summer after an interval of seventeen years, I was impressed anew with the beauty of her art, the magnificence of her architecture, and the splendor of her parks and gardens. Many examples of these are not only national but international treasures, for which France is trustee; their influence on the art of the world will always be full of inspiration.

That some of these great national monuments should be showing the devastating effects of time, because current repairs could not be kept up during the war, and that others should still bear silent witness to the ravages of war, stirred in me feelings of deep regret. I realize that this situation is only temporary and will eventually right itself as the people of France are able to turn from other and more pressing tasks and resume that scrupulous maintenance of their public monuments for which thay have established so enviable a reputation. In the meantime, I should count it a privilege to be allowed to help toward that end, and shall be happy to contribute one million dollars, its expenditure to be entrusted to a small committee composed of Frenchmen and Americans.

It would be my thought that this money should be used for the reconstruction of the roof of Rheims Cathedral; for the reconditioning of the buildings, fountains and gardens of Versailles; and for the purpose of making repairs that are urgently needed in the palace and gardens of Fontainebleau.

I am moved to make this proposal, not only because of my admiration for these great outstanding products of art, the influence of which should be continued unimpaired through the centuries to the enrichment of the lives of succeeding generations, but also because of the admiration which I have for the people of France, their fine spirit, their high courage, and their devotion to home life.

With sentiments of high regards, I am, my dear Mr. President,

Very sincerely,

JOHN D. ROCKEFELLER, JR.

I
Versailles and America
before
the twentieth century

France sets out to conquer America

The French
Crown and the
New World

In 1664, the great European powers were locked in conflict over this far-flung land of America, christened a century and a half earlier on a map printed at Saint-Dié in the Vosges, in honor of the explorer Amerigo Vespucci. The ports on America's eastern seaboard were now the prize in the rivalry between Dutch and English colonists, and in that same year an English fleet based in Boston returned victorious from the port of New Amsterdam, where it had successfully overcome the Dutch resistance. Peter Stuyvesant, the unpopular governor who had never been forgiven for imposing a nine o'clock curfew on the port in 1626, had surrendered to the British on 8 September 1664. New Holland was renamed New York by the victors, in honor of the Duke of York, brother of Charles II and new owner of the settlement.

On the other side of the Atlantic, another birth was being celebrated: that of Versailles. The French king, Louis XIV, invited courtiers and musicians, dancers and poets, his wife Queen Marie-Thérèse, and his mistress, the celebrated Mademoiselle de La Vallière, to discover the gardens designed by André le Nôtre, the initial outlines of the tremendous ensemble that was later to become the symbol of France's greatness. There he presented them with seven days of uninterrupted celebrations and entertainments, the famous *'Plaisirs de l'Ile enchantée'*. Nothing was too magnificent for this twenty-five-year-old king, who since 1643 had reigned over a land that was prosperous, industrious, successful, and — for a time — at peace with its Spanish, English, Austrian, and Dutch neighbors.
In 1661, Louis XIV had entrusted the architect Louis Le Vau with the task of enlarging and refurbishing in sumptuous style the simple hunting lodge

Jacques Cartier
discovers
the St Lawrence

France's interest in the New World stretched back before Versailles and the reign of Louis XIV to the early sixteenth century, when François I funded voyages by explorers such as Jacques Cartier, who discovered the St Lawrence River in Canada in 1535.

built at Versailles by his father, Louis XIII, from 1624. But before the first stone was laid of his new Italianate palace — on which work started only in 1668 — the king was determined to establish his dominion over the natural world, here too continuing a task already begun by his father, who had started to drain the marshy terrain.

Louis XIV chose the landscape designer who had created the gardens at Vaux-le-Vicomte, laid out in straight lines in a style later to become known as '*à la française*' which, like the château itself, was to exercise a remarkable degree of influence on modern taste. 'As night fell, an infinite number of chandeliers disposed against the tall green palisades, each holding twenty-four candles, together with two hundred torches of white wax held by as many masked figures, shed a light that was almost as luminous and more delightful than daylight,' recounted Molière, who contributed to the '*Plaisirs*' with a performance for the court of his latest comedy, *Tartuffe*. The composer Lully and his troupe, meanwhile, staged *La Princesse d'Elide* in 'a circle of greenery arranged as a theatre'. At the royal table, decked with flowers and set in gardens embellished with the unfortunate Fouquet's orange trees, brought from Vaux-le-Vicomte, the most exquisite delicacies were served. Fireworks and fountains added the final magnificent flourishes to this memorable inauguration.

Between the impenetrable virgin forests of North America and the modest hill of Versailles, there stretched an apparently infinite distance. And yet, since Christopher Columbus's discovery of 1492, the French had never ceased to turn their gaze westwards. Sailors from Saint-Malo, fishermen from Paimpol, Jesuit or foreign explorers in the service of the French king,

Map of Nouvelle-France

Colbert, minister to Louis XIV, was the moving force behind the colonization of Nouvelle-France during the last third of the seventeenth century. This map of *c.*1705 would appear to imply that the new colony encompassed virtually the whole of North America.

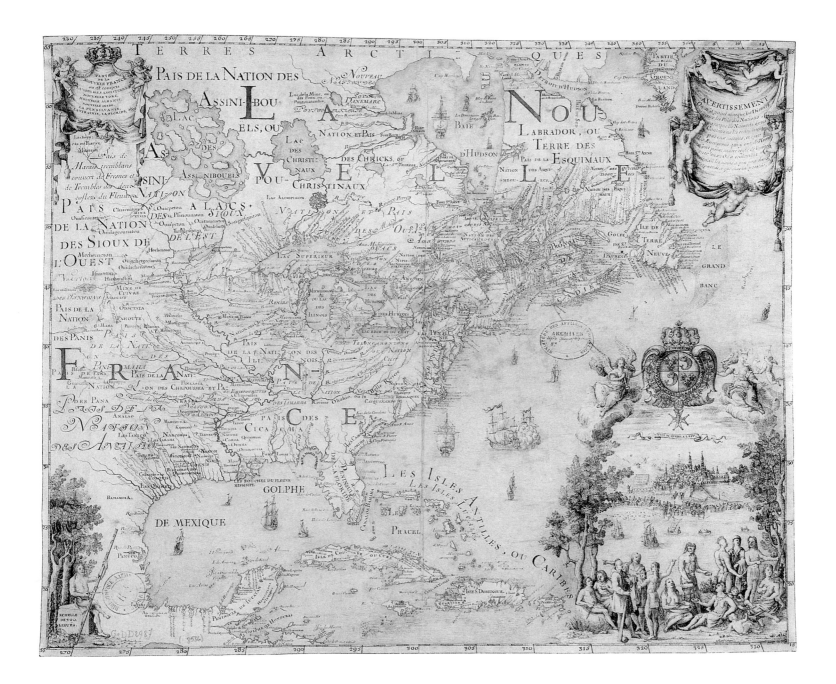

adventurers, Protestants fleeing persecution — all managed to conquer their fear of an ocean whose waters were believed to be infested with monsters in order to discover this 'Mundo Novus'.

As early as 1524, the Florentine navigator Giovanni da Verrazzano, sailing in the name of François I, the first French king to take an interest in the new continent, had entered the bay of New York aboard his ship *La Dauphine*: 'Sire,' he wrote on 8 July, 'we have named this land Angoulême, after the name borne by Your Majesty in a former, less exalted position.' Ten years later, Jacques Cartier was to discover the shores of Canada, erecting on the cliff of Gaspé on 24 July 'a gigantic cross with a sign bearing the fleur-de-lis'. And it was here in Canada in 1608, with the blessing of Henri IV, that Samuel Champlain established Nouvelle-France, the great French empire of the Americas. Encouraging settlers to make their homes along the banks of the St Lawrence River, he also forged the first alliances with the native Huron Indians. Peopling this new territory quickly became a priority, and it was with this aim in mind, and with a view to inspiring hesitant prospective emigrants, that in Paris in 1609 Marc Lescarbot published his *Histoire de la Nouvelle-France*, in which he painted an idyllic picture of the settlers' life. Cardinal Richelieu also provided encouragement, urging would-be colonists to set out not only for America and Canada but also for the West Indies, with their bounty of coffee, sugarcane, and indigo.
Later, Louis XIV's minister Jean-Baptiste Colbert persuaded the king to send a new expedition to Nouvelle-France and appointed a new governor, Jean Talon. In just over a decade, from 1663 to 1674, the number of new settlers rose from 2500 to 7000. In North America, the role of French

Playing cards of the young Louis XIV

In 1644, Cardinal Mazarin commissioned a set of playing cards designed to instruct the young Louis XIV in the rudiments of geography. As an indication of the growing importance of the New World, America featured alongside Florida, Virginia, and Nouvelle-France.

Amerique

Quatriesme partie du monde, découuerte
depuis 150 ans, autrement dicte, les Indes
Occidentales, ou le nouueau monde.
situeé vers l'Occident, et diuiseé en deux
grandes peninsules, l'vne appelleé
Amerique Mexicane, l'autre Peruane.
elle s'estend sur toutes les zones.

Nouuelle France

Comprend Canada, et s'estend le long
du fleuue St Laurens. Pays couuert
d'arbres, et mal cultiué. En suite est
au Nort la Terre neuue, la terre du
Laboureur, et Estotiland.

---

missionaries was of fundamental importance, for while the Amerindian fur trade was profitable to France, the French monarchy did not attempt to conceal its desire to 'Frenchify' the indigenous peoples — that is, to convert them to Catholicism. The antechambers to the French court, thronged by the nation's scholars, geographers, and men of letters, were avid for tales of these intrepid missionaries' voyages, which before long rivalled novels in popularity. Thus in 1664, the Parisian publisher Cramoisy published a volume by one Jérôme Lallemand entitled *Accounts of the most remarkable experiences of the Missions of the Fathers of the Company of Jesus in Nouvelle-France in the years 1662 and 1663*. As Montaigne observed in his *Essays*: 'The Old World found itself confronted with a New World which even the Sybil had not predicted.' What did the New World look like to these newcomers?

First encounters

'The people go quite naked, men and women, just as their mothers brought them into the world. They have no iron, no steel, no weapons; nor are they suited for such things; not because they are not well made and tall enough,

American characters
in the Carrousel of 1662

Even before serving as a theme for entertainments at Versailles, America featured in lavish fashion in the carrousel staged by command of Louis XIV at the Tuileries on 3, 4, and 5 June 1662, in celebration of the birth of the Dauphin. Dressed as their king, Louis XIV's cousin headed a cavalcade of American characters in picturesque costumes.

Escuyer et Page Ameriquains

but rather because they are marvelously timorous ... They are naïve and generous with their possessions, to a degree that only those who have witnessed it would believe.'[1]

Such were the terms chosen by Christopher Columbus to describe the inhabitants of the New World in a letter to Ferdinand and Isabella of Spain, dated 15 February to 14 March 1493. In his quest for the Indies, the explorer had discovered a new continent — and one that proved, moreover, to be inhabited. At the end of his first voyage, Columbus brought a few of the indigenous people back to Spain with him: 'On 31 March 1493, Palm Sunday, the Admiral and his entourage made a thrilling entrance into Seville, accompanied by six Indians brought back from the islands who were garbed in ceremonial dress, decked out with arms and gold ornaments and carrying parrots in cages.'

The first Indian to enter France disembarked at Honfleur in 1505. Brought back from Brazil by Captain Binot Paulmier de Gonneville, he was known by the name of Essomericq and was to make his home in France, marrying a local girl and founding a flourishing Amerindian-Norman dynasty. The vogue, if so it may be called, was launched, and the inhabitants of the New World assumed the status of a highly prized diversion. At the French court it was fashionable to include an Amerindian among one's entourage, such as the young boy who served as a companion to the Dauphin at the château of Saint-Germain.

In 1613, Louis XIII received a delegation of visitors from the New World, consisting of six Brazilian Tupinamba Indians dressed in feathers: 'Thirty-six Capuchin brothers accompanied them. The dignitaries of Paris flocked

Cartoon for 'America' on the Ambassadors' Staircase

The Ambassadors' Staircase, built from 1674 by the architect François d'Orbay to designs by Le Vau, was the ceremonial staircase at Versailles and one of the palace's most sumptuous interiors. The *trompe l'œil* wall paintings by Charles Le Brun included a scene depicting 'the different nations of America', featuring an Indian and seven European colonists.

Indian costume
for a ballet performance

In the second half of
the seventeenth century,
the New World also
provided inspiration
for opera librettists and
set designers, as for
example in this design for
an Indian costume by
Jean Bérain.

Bureau brisé, 1685

A small desk with folding top (*bureau brisé*) by Oppenord, once part of the furnishings of Louis XIV's Petit Cabinet at Versailles, donated to the Metropolitan Museum of Art in New York by Mrs. Charles Wrightsman.

Table, *c.*1670

A rare table in ivory
veneer and stained horn,
possibly made for the
Trianon de Porcelaine
at Versailles and
now in the J. Paul Getty
Museum in Los Angeles.

to see them in such great numbers that the Capuchins were obliged to withdraw to the safety of their monastery with their exotic flock.' Three of the latter were baptized, wearing costumes of white taffeta and feathered hats for the ceremony, and holding lilies in their hands.

The growth of French settlements in Canada, in the Maritime Provinces and on the banks of the St Lawrence River was to intensify these exchanges. The Jesuits, both explorers and missionaries, sent Amerindian children to France in order to accelerate their conversion to the Catholic faith.

In 1638, one of these young Canadian Indians was presented to Louis XIII. At the king's feet he placed as a gift his crown of 'wampum' and his shells, which served among the Amerindians as money, 'as a mark of his recognition in the name of all his peoples of this great Prince as their true and legitimate Monarch'. In return, the king and queen presented him with costumes of 'cloth of gold, velvet, satin, silk velvet, and scarlatine', which the young boy took back with him to Nouvelle-France. In their turn, the chiefs of his tribe sent the Dauphin, the future Louis XIV, an Amerindian costume: 'By this we do not intend a gift, for he [the king] has riches far greater than ours, but a "metawagan", a modest toy to entertain his young son, who may perhaps be amused to see the manner in which our children are dressed.'[2]

This French passion for the exoticism of America was manifested in unusually colorful fashion. In 1662, for example, at a carrousel staged at the Tuileries on 3, 4, and 5 June to celebrate the birth of the Dauphin, the king's cousin the Duc de Guise led a cavalcade of 'Americans' garbed in costumes that were as extravagant as they were picturesque.

The Nymph of Dampierre

Following the demolition of the Ambassadors' Staircase in 1752, its marbles were sent to the stores of the Bâtiments du Roi, before in some cases being used again elsewhere. Part of the fountain that originally stood on the central landing was reused by the Duc de Chevreuse in his château at Dampierre, with this nymph by the sculptor Vassé, which he had exhibited at the Salon of 1761.

Cherubs playing with a Swan

Two sculptures from the Théâtre d'Eau at Versailles are now in the National Gallery of Art in Washington D.C. This one by Jean-Baptiste Tuby dates from the 1670s.

Cherubs playing with a Lyre

Pierre Legros made this lead sculpture for the bosquet known as the Théâtre d'Eau, one of the first such features to be completed in the gardens at Versailles after 1671.

The vogue

for America

at Versailles

The exoticism of the New World also flourished at Versailles, where the Sun King had decided to establish his court. On 23 March 1668, for instance, 'Louis XIV went to Versailles for an entertainment on the lake featuring a number of gilded boats… There too were some Iroquois in their canoes brought from the Indies, carved from a single piece of wood, which they paddled with extraordinary speed.'[3] Not merely did their skill at paddling arouses the admiration of the court, but also their ability to make fire using two pieces of wood, as had already been demonstrated before Henri IV at the château of Fontainebleau. The elements of fire and water, both so dear to Louis XIV, added a further note of glamor to the sumptuous entertainments staged at Versailles, tales of which fascinated both the French people and all the courts of Europe.

'We are quite delighted at Versailles; each day brings new pleasures, plays, concerts, and suppers on water… We ply the canal in gondolas to the strains of music; we return at ten o'clock; we go to the play; midnight strikes and we have a midnight feast,' recounted Madame de Sévigné, that assiduous observer of court life, in her *Letters*. In 1664, it was the *'Plaisirs de l'Ile enchantée'* that set the tone, followed by the 'great royal entertainment' of 18 July 1668 and the lavish diversions of the summer of 1674, when 'the shimmering of the waters vied in brilliance and beauty with that of the torchlight and the murmuring of the fountains echoed the sighing of the violins.' For the diversion of a court accustomed to constant entertainments, new and ever more astonishing spectacles were required. With mythology remaining a recurrent theme, the New World offered the requisite degree of novelty.

America in the park
at Versailles

This allegorical sculpture by Gilles Guérin, a collaborator of Charles Le Brun, stands on the North Parterre in the park at Versailles. It depicts a female figure wearing a feathered head-dress and with at her feet a crocodile, an animal which made frequent appearances in early representations of the New World.

In the Old World, the New World was represented initially by the myth of the noble savage, which proved irresistible to writers, librettists, and decorative artists alike. In entertainments, the arrival of the *'ballets indiens'* was invariably greeted with enthusiastic applause. At the Théâtre Royal in 1703, the audience was captivated by the character of Adario, the Huron Indian 'of good sense and considerable travels' who engaged the author, the Baron de La Hontan, in conversation. Simultaneously, the age of discovery and the tales brought back by explorers initiated a second representation of this distant continent of America.

In the French imagination, America remained a land of mystery that was in itself sufficient justification for every type of experience or experiment. Learned minds at the University of Montpellier devoted themselves to the solemn question of whether or not 'the flesh of venomous animals poisons those who eat it'. Jean de Léry, a Huguenot minister, tasted lizard flesh and pronounced it excellent; Jean Moquet, geographer to Henri IV, tried crocodile meat and found it tasteless. Those avid for new experiences sampled fruits brought from the New World, such as the pineapples discovered in Brazil by Jean de Léry in 1555, and which Louis XV was to put into cultivation at Versailles in 1733. In the wake of the potato, which made its first appearance in Europe in 1534, came peanuts, dubbed 'earth pistachios', aubergines, haricot beans, and of course maize. Bananas, cocoa, coffee, and sugarcane were all served at the royal table. And as often as not these strange plants were believed to be panaceas for all ills, like the quinquina or 'Jesuit powder' for which Louis XIV purchased the secret recipe from the Englishman Talbot in 1679.

Char de Triomphe tapestry

In 1717, the Gobelins tapestry workshop delivered to the Garde-meuble de la Couronne this portière bearing the royal arms of France and Navarre, now in the J. Paul Getty Museum in Los Angeles.

An allegorical

vision of America

By the late seventeenth century, almost two centuries after the discovery of the New World, America still remained an allegorical vision, peopled by noble savages who inhabited a lost paradise. In 1638 a collection of engravings entitled *Historic America* was published, with a frontispiece depicting a couple dressed in feathers and standing before a scene of cannibalism: somehow the court of Louis XIV, with all its rouge and powder, its preposterous wigs and extravagant costumes, contrived to reconcile itself with this world of nakedness and cannibalism. 'For artists, the discovery of peoples who lived in a state of nature coincided with a return in taste to classicism and antiquity, to the pastoral idyll of earliest times and the cult of physical beauty.'[4] As for the thorny problem of cannibalism, in his *Essays*, published in 1580, Montaigne partly absolved these 'Cannibals' — or 'bold' men in the Caribbean language — who ate human flesh but did not (unlike Europeans) inflict torture on one another.

Feathers, nakedness, and cannibalism thus became the distinguishing characteristics of the American savage. 'On frontispieces to atlases, to albums of costumes and to volumes devoted to natural history and pharmacopoeias, on map cartouches and in stage sets and collections of ornamental engravings, "America" was embodied by a young naked woman, endowed by artists according to taste with long tresses, floating free or caught up in a chignon, crowned with a diadem or a head-dress of feathers, pearls, precious stones or gold beads, and armed with a javelin and bow and arrow. Accompanying her was invariably a many-coloured macaw, a sea turtle or a modest-sized alligator.'[5] A striking example of this convention may be seen today in Gilles Guérin's seventeenth-century statue which stands, complete with alligator, on the North Parterre at Versailles.

The Duchess of Parma and her daughter

In 1750, the painter Nattier sent this portrait of Madame Infante, beloved daughter of Louis XV, to Versailles, before it was dispatched to the Duchess in Italy. It may now be seen in Washington D.C., in the Hillwood Museum founded by Marjorie Merriweather-Post, herself a benefactor of Versailles.

Spring by Boucher

In *c.*1750, François Boucher painted for the Marquise de Pompadour a set of *dessus-de-porte* depicting the four seasons, purchased in 1916 by Henry Clay Frick for his house in New York.

The vogue for American exotica was now at its height. Collectors seized upon it as a new subject for their collections; in the king's cabinet of curiosities, for instance, were assembled 'the clothes, weapons and tools of newly discovered peoples', the earliest of which came from the collections of François I. Instead of the gold so eagerly coveted by their patrons, explorers returned from their expeditions bearing examples of the everyday objects — hammocks, porcelain necklaces, moccasins, bags, and belts — of the Amerindians. Not surprisingly, such objects served as a source of inspiration for the artists working on the décor at Versailles: 'the ceiling is richly decorated with all sorts of weapons, equipment, and clothes used by savages… as well as four large aprons or coats of painted skins in the manner of the Illinois Indians.'[6] Nor was the king the only one to possess this type of souvenir. The famous set of tapestries entitled *Les Indes*, woven at the Gobelins in about 1690, was inspired by paintings by Post and Eckhout from the 'American' — in fact Brazilian — collection of Comte Maurice de Nassau-Siegen, which he had presented to Louis XIV in 1678.[7] To all these curiosities were soon to be added trophies from the French conquest of the valley of the Mississippi.

Versailles and 'Louis-iana'

Thanks to the influence of Jean-Baptiste Colbert, the Sun King's comptroller of finances who was as valued for his loyalty as he was detested for his repeated criticisms of the extravagances of court expenditure, France continued her conquest of the New World. Funds were now raised for further expeditions, such as those of Marquette and Joliet, who navigated the Mississippi, and of the settler Cavelier de La Salle, who in 1682 sailed down this mighty river to found the colony of Louisiana: 'We have named this great

Painting and Sculpture and *Architecture and Chemistry*

The panels painted by Boucher for Madame de Pompadour's library at Crécy symbolize the importance of her role as a patron of the arts during the years 1745-60, when she was mistress to Louis XV. They are now in the Frick Collection in New York.

discovery Louisiana, being persuaded that Your Majesty would not dis-approve of this region of the Earth watered by a river over eight hundred leagues in length and far larger than Europe … and which is capable of for-ming a great Empire henceforth being known by the august name of Louis… It would appear, Sire, that it is God's design that Your Majesty should be master of this land, for there is a happy consonance between your glorious name and the sun, which the people here call in their language Louis, and to which, as a mark of their respect and adoration, before smok-ing they present their pipes with the words, *"Tchendouba Louis"*, meaning "smoke sun". Thus Your Majesty's name is at all times on their lips, for they do nothing without first paying homage to the sun under this name of Louis.'[8]

In May 1684, the 'Compagnie des Indes occidentales', or West India Company founded by La Salle at Versailles, was awarded the monopoly on trade 'in the islands and mainland of America', and in 1687 the explorer mounted a second expedition, which he was not to survive. Just over a decade later, in 1699, Louis XIV sent in his wake Pierre Lemoyne d'Iberville and his brother Jean-Baptiste, who were finally to discover the mouth of the Mississippi that had eluded La Salle, and who founded a settlement there.

In 1699 they founded Fort Maurepas, to be followed in 1716 by Fort Rosalie, on the site of the Natchez Indian settlement. The Natchez Indians were also sun-worshippers: 'Every morning as the sun appears, the great

America

In 1760, Jean-Jacques Bachelier painted for the château of Choisy, residence of Louis XV, a canvas entitled *America* in which the New World was symbolized by a variety of exotic birds, not all of which were American natives, despite the artist's efforts at authenticity.

Californian lizard

While scientific exactitude was not always a matter of great importance to artists, scientists by contrast could hardly contain their fascination for these unexplored lands. In 1768, Abbé Chappe d'Auteroche, himself an astronomer, undertook a voyage to California, taking with him Pauly, 'geographer and engineer to the king', and the artist Noël, who made this drawing.

Chief stands at the door of his hut, turns to the East and utters three cries, prostrating himself on the ground. He is then brought a pipe which is used only for this purpose. He smokes it, blowing the tobacco smoke in the direction of the morning star… He recognizes no master on Earth except the sun… He exercises unlimited power over his subjects and may dispose of their possessions and their lives.'[9] The ceremonial that surrounded the supreme chief of the Natchez, the Great Sun, as described by Charlevoix and immortalized in an engraving by Bossu, is curiously reminiscent of the rigid organization that governed the king's 'Grand Lever' at Versailles, as described by the Duc de Saint-Simon: 'As soon as he was dressed, he [Louis XIV] went to pray to God beside his bed, where all the clergy present went down on their knees, the cardinals with their heads bared; the laymen remained standing and the captain of the guard came to the baluster during prayers, after which the King went into his cabinet.'[10]

Commode by Joubert, 1769

A commode
by the cabinetmaker
Gilles Joubert,
delivered to Versailles
for Madame Louise
de France, youngest
daughter of Louis XV.
In the nineteenth century
it belonged to the
Rothschild family; it is
now in the J. Paul Getty
Museum in Los Angeles.

Sketch for
L'Amérique septentrionale

In 1759, Louis XV
declared, 'Every part
of the world has played
its part and taken
its turn. Soon it will be
the turn of America!'
Three years later, for
the offices of the Ministry
of Foreign Affairs
at Versailles, Bachelier
painted a canvas
depicting North America
which attests to the
importance invested
in these colonies by the
French crown.

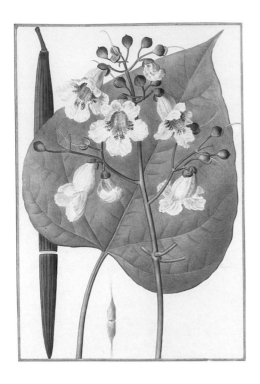

View of the Queen's
Hamlet at Trianon

When he visited the
gardens of the
Petit Trianon in 1787,
the British traveller
Arthur Young
observed American
native species including
swamp cypresses
(*Taxodium distichum*),
tulip trees
(*Liriodendron tulipifera*),
and American red oaks
(*Quercus rubra*).

Bignonia catalpa
Rhododendron maximum
Pinus strobus
Liriodendron tulipifera

European understanding
of America became more
sophisticated during
the reign of Louis XVI,
who took a keen interest
in geography and
the sciences. In the 1780s,
he funded an expedition
to North America by
the distinguished
botanists André Michaux
and his son François.
The botanical
illustrations on vellum
carried out on their
return now form part
of the remarkable
collections of the library
of the Muséum d'Histoire
Naturelle in Paris.

To people the colony of Louisiana, young French women were sent over, the most celebrated of whom was the fictional Manon Lescaut, created by Abbé Prévost in 1731, while the Natchez Indians were to provide an exotic background for François-René de Chateaubriand's novel *Atala*, published in 1801.

On 31 August 1715, Louis XIV died at Versailles, leaving behind him a growing American empire that was almost exclusively French. With him there perished a notion of the monarchy, splendid and absolute, as symbolized by the great palace and park that he had so loved, the work of artists of the calibre of Louis Le Vau, Jules Hardouin-Mansart, André Le Nôtre and Charles Le Brun. When the five-year-old Louis XV succeeded to the French throne he left Versailles, to return seven years later. There he was to complete the project begun by his great-grandfather in the Hercules Salon (Salon d'Hercule), which linked the chapel and the state apartments; he also built the Royal Opera and would have liked to give form to Jules Hardouin-Mansart's 'Grand Dessein'. But by 1763 the state coffers were empty. The Seven Years War (1756-63), fought out by France and Britain in the New World and known by the Americans as the French and Indian War, had drained the royal treasury dry. In that same year, the Treaty of Paris put an end to the war. France lost Canada and its remaining territories in Louisiana, keeping only its West Indian colonies of Martinique, Guadeloupe, and Saint Pierre et Miquelon.

America

Allegorical representations of America barely changed during the course of the eighteenth century, despite growing knowledge of the land itself. This drawing by Vestier displays the conventional attributes, including a feathered head-dress and tunic made from panther skins.

France champions the United States

On 5 September 1774, in this land of America that was now in the full throes of development, came the first meeting of a Congress made up of representatives of the thirteen colonies. Patrick Henry delivered a speech in which he insisted that there no longer existed any distinction between Virginians, Pennsylvanians, New Yorkers, and New Englanders, culminating with the ringing phrase: 'I am not a Virginian but an American.'[11] In the face of constantly increasing import duties imposed by Britain, the settlers resorted to sabotage: on 16 December 1773 the port of Boston was the scene of an attack that became known as the Boston Tea Party, when colonists disguised as Indians overran three East India Company tea clippers and hurled their cargo of tea into the sea.

In 1775, war broke out between Great Britain and America, and George Washington took command of the colonist forces. On his return from England, Benjamin Franklin found his countrymen ready to fight for their freedom at all costs. A year later, Thomas Paine drew up a forty-seven page document entitled *Common Sense*, which was to inspire the Declaration of Independence, signed on 4 July and published two days later in the Pennsylvania *Evening Post*. It included the first reference to the United States of America.

At Versailles, Louis XV had just died of smallpox. He was succeeded by Louis XVI, the last absolute French monarch before the abolition of royal privileges. Aged only twenty, the new king and his even younger queen, Marie-Antoinette, were to bring a breath of fresh air to the sumptuous palace of his forebears. The queen decorated the Petit Trianon and built her famous Hamlet, where she delighted in the 'simple' bucolic pleasures of life as a dairymaid.

The Marquis
de La Fayette

Descendant of an ancient family that had served the crown since the fifteenth century, Gilbert du Motier, Marquis de La Fayette, was the first member of the French aristocracy to be fired by the cause of freedom for the American colonies. His numerous connections at court at Versailles were to help to win over Louis XVI's ministers and finally the king himself.

The Comte de Vergennes

The treaty putting an end to the Seven Years War in 1763 was disastrous for France, now inferior in power to England. Senior state officials such as the Comte de Vergennes, Minister of Foreign Affairs under Louis XVI, viewed French support of the American revolution as an opportunity to take revenge on the British crown.

Although the Treaty of Paris of 1763 had deprived France of most of its North American territories, French interest in America continued unabated, for as Louis XV had predicted in 1759, 'Every part of the world has played its part and taken its turn. Soon it will be the turn of America!' At Versailles, the French crown — awaiting an opportunity to take its revenge — viewed the agitation in the colonies as propitious. Sharing this view, Comte Charles Gravier de Vergennes, Minister for Foreign Affairs, dispatched one of his emissaries, Achard de Bonvouloir, to America.

American supporters of independence, though desperately short of money, turned only with reluctance to France, for the years of French colonization had not left them with happy memories. 'People do not like the French,' recounted an American soldier in his memoirs: ' when they meet men whom they dislike, they call them French.' The French were associated with the Jesuits and with the Catholic faith, viewed by the Americans as obscurantist. The government at Versailles, meanwhile, was decried — not without justice — as the embodiment of tyranny and despotism. But France was the most populous country in Europe, with twenty-five million inhabitants, and it already harbored genuinely pro-American sentiments.

By September 1776, these two reasons were deemed sufficient justification for America to send three emissaries to France: Benjamin Franklin, Silas Deane, and Arthur Lee. The Comte de Beaumarchais, author of *The Barber of Seville* and *The Marriage of Figaro*, was now made responsible for organizing clandestine aid to the colonies. Advised to set up a private company, Hortalez & Cie, which would supply the Americans with weapons and munitions in return for the Virginia tobacco of which Louis XVI was so fond, the man of letters thus found himself transformed into an arms dealer.

La Fayette embarks for America

With a large fortune at his disposal, La Fayette personally chartered a vessel to transport to America arms, munitions and officers wishing to support the colonist troops. The *Victoire* sailed from the port of Los Pasajes, close to San Sebastian, on 26 April 1777, arriving within sight of the coast of South Carolina on 13 June.

He also had several meetings at Versailles with Louis XVI and his minister Vergennes, during which he attempted to persuade them to send aid to the colonies.

At the same time, pro-American sympathies began to stir in France, with the first signs appearing at Versailles. Aristocrats such as the nineteen-year-old Gilbert du Motier, Marquis de La Fayette, the Comte de Ségur, the Duc de Lauzun, the Marquis and the Vicomte de Vaudreuil and the Comte de Rochambeau decided to forsake court life in order to lend their support to the independence movement. Under the management of Beaumarchais, meanwhile, Hortalez & Cie acquired a fleet of ships in order to assure essential supplies to the colonists.

The decisive victory of George Washington's army at Saratoga in 1777 finally overcame the resistance of the French king, who until then had still hesitated to provide direct funding for the American war effort against the British. At Versailles, a few days after Vergennes conveyed news of the victory of 7 October to him, Louis XVI signed a note expressing his favorable attitude to possible contacts with an American delegation.

Benjamin Franklin at Versailles

Successive Louis might come and go, but the Hall of Mirrors (Galerie des Glaces) at Versailles, with its seventeen great windows, its monumental arcade of seventeen mirrors and its barrel-vaulted ceiling painted by Le Brun, remained unchanged. It was in this gallery, dubbed by Madame de Sevigné 'a royal beauty unique in the world', that on 20 March 1778 preparations were completed for the reception of Dr. Benjamin Franklin, 'envoy extraordinary and plenipotentiary of the young Republic of thirteen States to the court of His Most Christian Majesty'. For Benjamin Franklin, who had

Commode by Roentgen

This commode, in marquetry embellished with gilt bronze mounts and bearing the marks of the palace of Versailles, now forms part of the Linsky Collection at the Metropolitan Museum of Art in New York.

Benjamin Franklin

On 6 February 1778, in the name of his newly born country, Benjamin Franklin signed a treaty of friendship, trade, and alliance by which France recognized the existence of an independent United States. For the French, Franklin was the embodiment of a mythical and legendary America, replete with every virtue. Great artists vied with each other for the honor of painting his portrait.

Reception of Benjamin Franklin at Versailles

On 20 March 1778, Louis XVI received Benjamin Franklin in ceremony at Versailles. After presenting him to the king, the Comte de Vergennes, French Minister of Foreign Affairs, observed of the scholarly American: 'Only the man who discovered electricity could have electrified the opposite ends of the earth.'

The Hôtel de Valentinois

During their mission to France, Franklin and the other members of the American delegation, Arthur Lee, Silas Deane, and John Adams, stayed at the Hôtel de Valentinois, overlooking the Seine. This was also the setting for Franklin's first experiments with electricity.

been in France, at Passy, since the month of December, and for the delegates who accompanied him, this was a powerfully symbolic day, marking the first official act of diplomacy of the American nation.

Since his arrival in France a few months earlier, Benjamin Franklin, discoverer of electricity and inventor of the lightning conductor, had attracted crowds wherever he went. As John Adams observed, 'Franklin's fame was universal. His name was familiar to government and people, to kings, courtiers and nobility, clergy and philosophers as well as plebeians to such a degree that there was scarcely a peasant or a citizen, a valet de chambre, coachman or footman, a lady's chambermaid or a scullion in a kitchen who was not familiar with it and who did not consider him as a friend to human kind.'[12]

In Paris as at court, this seventy-year-old scientist and diplomat who read French and spoke it a little was a source of fascination. Franklin became something of a cult figure, with his portrait appearing on hats, shirts, rings, bracelets, and snuffboxes. It even became fashionable to dress one's hair

Pair of Sèvres vases

In 1779, the Sèvres manufactory delivered to Versailles this pair of vases painted by Antoine Caton, now in the Museum of Fine Arts in Boston.

Set of three Sèvres vases

This set of three Sèvres vases from Louis XVI's library, by Antoine Caton, Philippe Parpette, and Etienne-Henri Leguay, is now in the J. Paul Getty Museum in Los Angeles.

'*à la Franklin*', with wigs imitating the shape of the curious fur hat that he always wore, a purchase brought back from his last visit to Canada. He himself described his singular appearance as 'very plainly dressed, wearing my thin, gray straight hair, that peeps out under my only coiffure, a fine fur cap, which comes down my forehead almost to my spectacles'. And the Comte de Ségur noted the picturesque figure that he cut in French high society: 'Nothing was more striking than the great contrast between the luxury of our capital, the elegance of our fashions, the magnificence of Versailles, the living evidence of the royal splendor of Louis XIV and the polished dignity of our refined aristocracy, and the almost rustic attire, the simple but proud bearing, the free and direct language, the undressed, unpowdered hair, and finally that ancient air which seemed suddenly to bring within our walls, among the weak and servile civilization of the eighteenth century, the wise contemporaries of Plato or republicans of the times of Cato and Fabius.'[13]

In March 1778, Benjamin Franklin and his compatriots, Silas Deane, Ralph Izard, Arthur Lee, and his brother William, came to Versailles to witness the ratification by Louis XVI of treaties of alliance and trade which the proud new American nation, strong in the confidence of its Declaration of Independence, had signed with France on 6 February: 'the first treaty of alliance ever signed by the United States, and the only one until the North Atlantic Treaty of 1949'.[14] For the occasion, Franklin had been prepared to make an exception to his legendary simplicity: he ordered a wig, but at the last moment swapped it for a round-brimmed grey hat, finally appearing 'in a dark, plain-colored costume, with the inevitable ruffles at the collar and

The 'Independence' coiffure

Court ladies at Versailles also took up the cause of American independence, sporting elaborate coiffures inspired by the naval confrontations between the French and English fleets off the coast of Brittany in 1778.

50

Cœffure à l'Indépendance ou le Triomphe de la liberté.

George Washington

For the French, the third figure of quasi-mythical status in the cause of American independence — alongside Franklin and Jefferson — was George Washington, who in turn was seduced by La Fayette's enthusiasm for the colonists' cause.

John Paul Jones

One of the few
Americans to have
fought against
England off the French
coast, John Paul Jones
was decorated with
the order of military merit
by Louis XVI.
The king even decided
to fund from his own
private purse
the fitting out of a small
squadron in which
the American admiral set
sail in August 1779.

The Marquis de Ségur

Minister of War under
Louis XVI,
the Marquis de Ségur
lent his support to
the Comte de Vergennes,
Minister of Foreign
Affairs, the Comte
de Maurepas, President
of the Council of State,
and M. de Sartine
and later the Marquis
de Castries, Ministers
of the Navy, in the
organization of the War
of Independence.

The Comte
de Rochambeau

An older and more
experienced soldier than
La Fayette, the Comte
de Rochambeau was
appointed by Louis XVI
to command the French
expeditionary force
sent in 1780 to support
the Americans in their
struggle for independence.

cuffs, white silk stockings and gold buckles'. He was the talk of the town. Madame Campan described the scene: 'His flat, unpowdered hair, his round-brimmed hat and his costume of brown cloth contrasted with the sequinned and embroidered costumes and the powdered and perfumed wigs of the courtiers at Versailles. This novelty charmed all the lively minds among the French ladies.'[15] In the Œil de Bœuf Salon (Salon de l'Œil de Bœuf), the antechamber to royal audiences, these court ladies were able to comment at their leisure upon the American visitor's curious appearance. Madame Vigée-Lebrun added: 'Had it not been for his noble countenance I should have taken him for a rough country squire, so great a contrast did he make with the other diplomats, who were all powdered, in court dress and smothered with gold and ribbons.'

From the Hall of Mirrors, the Americans were escorted directly to the King's State Bedchamber, the same room in which Louis XIV had died, which Louis XV had occupied in turn, and in which, eleven years later,

Robinson House, Newport, Rhode Island

The French troops under Rochambeau's command were stationed at Newport during the winter of 1780-1, where they were billeted on the local population. The Vicomte de Noailles thus found accommodation with the Robinson family in their house on Washington Street.

The Vicomte de Noailles

Son of Field Marshal
the Duc de Mouchy,
the Vicomte de Noailles
belonged to one of the
most illustrious families
at the French court.
Liberal in spirit, like
his brother-in-law
La Fayette, he joined
the first French
expeditionary force
sent to America
under Rochambeau's
command in 1780.

The Siege of Yorktown

Encircled in the fortified
settlement of Yorktown —
by the French fleet in
Chesapeake Bay and by
American and French
infantry on the landward
side — the English troops
under the command
of General Cornwallis
were forced to surrender
on 19 October 1781.

Louis XVI would present himself to the mob for the last time. Amid this panelled décor with its imposing bed hangings of heavy gold brocade and its three canvases by Valentin depicting the *Four Evangelists*, the *Denarius of Caesar* and the *Fortune-Teller* (now in the Louvre), the king received America. The interview was brief. Minister Vergennes presented the four Americans to His Majesty, whereupon the king addressed them thus: 'Gentlemen, I hope that this will prove to be to the good of both nations; I desire you to assure Congress of my friendship. I beg you also to inform it that I have been most satisfied with your comportment during your stay in my kingdom.' Benjamin Franklin thanked the king, adding: 'Your Majesty may count on the gratitude of Congress and on its loyalty to the commitments it makes.' With these words, France was to enter a war that was to cost it too dear, but it was also to gain a historic ally which on more than one occasion was to demonstrate the loyalty of its friendship.

This visit by Benjamin Franklin was the first in a long series. In September 1778, indeed, he was appointed minister plenipotentiary at the court of Versailles, and in this capacity presented himself at the palace every Tuesday. At Versailles, Benjamin Franklin noted that: 'the range of building is immense, the Garden Front most magnificient all of hewn stone... but the Waterworks are out of repair so is a great part of the Front next the Town, looking with its shabby half Brick Walls and Broken Windows not much better that the houses in Durham Yard. There is in short both at Versailles and Paris a Prodigious Mixture and Magnificence and Negligence with every kind of Elegance except that of cleanliness and what we call Tidyness.'[16] His popularity in France was now at its height. Jean-Baptiste Houdon

56

The Departure

In *The Departure*, the painter Wille chose a highly topical subject. For in the wake of La Fayette, there were few young French officers in love with glory — and with freedom — who did not dream of going to fight for Louis XVI against the English in America.

carved his portrait bust, and at the Louvre he posed for Fragonard for 'an allegory depicting America personified by a seated woman protected from a thunderbolt by the shield of Minerva, brandished by Franklin'. Louis XVI himself followed the fashion, 'presenting to the Comtesse de Polignac a handsome chamber pot with Franklin's physiognomy'.[17]

Versailles and the War of Independence

The war, supposed to be so swiftly won, dragged on. Three years after the signature of the treaty of alliance, France — at the persuasion of the Marquis de La Fayette — took the decision to send a French fleet.

On 9 October 1781, the siege of Yorktown, at which Frenchmen such as La Fayette, the Comte de Rochambeau and Admiral the Comte de Grasse distinguished themselves at the side of General George Washington, proved a turning point for the American colonists. Vergennes, on receiving news of the victory a month later, wrote to Benjamin Franklin: 'The English forces who held Yorktown emerged on 19 October with the honors of war in order to lay down their arms as prisoners. Some six thousand soldiers, eighteen hundred sailors, twenty-two standards and one hundred and seventy cannon — of which seventy-five are of bronze — are the trophies signalling this victory.'[18]

On 27 February, the British House of Commons voted to end the war. French troops remained in the field a few months longer before embarking for Boston, where they learned of the birth of Louis XVI's first child, the Dauphin, on 22 October 1781. On hearing this news, His Majesty's soldiers posted at West Point decided to build a pavilion of greenery inspired by the ephemeral constructions erected by the Menus Plaisirs for court entertainments at Versailles. To celebrate the event, so essential for the

Arbor at West Point

On 31 May 1782, French troops still stationed in America celebrated the birth of the Dauphin, son of Louis XVI. At West Point, they constructed an arbor formed from a colonnade of 118 wooden pillars surrounding a ballroom, in which General George Washington joined the festivities.

Proclamation of the Treaty of Paris in 1783

Popular rejoicing greeted the publication of the peace treaty — signed at Versailles but known as the Treaty of Paris — between France, England and the United States, officially enshrining American independence.

future of the dynasty, the Chevalier de La Luzerne, French minister in Philadelphia, organized major celebrations the following July, at which George Washington and General the Comte de Rochambeau were present, in a pavilion built by Pierre-Charles l'Enfant, future architect of the federal capital.

For France, the final cost of the American War of Independence, or Revolutionary War, was to prove extremely high. In Paris, Gouverneur Morris, the representative of the Philadelphia businessmen Robert Morris (to whom he was not related), succeeded in obtaining a cash loan from France of half a million dollars, which was invested in the brand new Bank of North America. Thus Louis XVI sent men, weapons, and money, all of which he himself desperately needed. At the end of his reign, the serious deficit in the royal finances had worsened. 'The annual deficit stood at over 100 million francs and repayment of the debt had grown to an alarming 250 million a year.'[19] Historians were later to observe that France's funding of the American War of Independence could well have contributed to the fall of the monarchy.

The third of September 1783 was the day of the signing of treaties. In Paris, at the Hôtel d'York, England (in the person of Sir David Hartley) recognized the independence of the thirteen American states (New Hampshire, Massachusetts, Rhode Island, Connecticut, New York, New Jersey, Pennsylvania, Delaware, Maryland, Virginia, North and South Carolina, and Georgia), while at Versailles the definitive treaty, or 'Peace of Paris' was signed in the presence of the Comte de Vergennes. The territory of the new nation of America henceforth extended from Florida in the south to

Louis XVI
and Benjamin Franklin

In the 1780s, the Niderviller manufactory in Lorraine produced a group of biscuit figurines symbolizing the gift of independence by Louis XVI to America, personified by Benjamin Franklin.

L'Amérique indépendante

In 1783, the successful conclusion of the War of Independence contributed significantly to the personal glory of Louis XVI who had supported it. Charles de Wailly's design for an obelisk to be erected at Port-Vendres thus depicts *L'Amérique indépendante*: a royal frigate carrying to the Americans assembled on the shores of Boston the Treaty of Independence.'

France champions the United States

Canada in the north. France, meanwhile, received Senegal and the West Indian island of Tobago.

French soldiers who had fought at Washington's side — and whose descendants now form the Order of Cincinnati[20] and the Sons of the American Revolution — were accorded a hero's welcome on their return to France. La Fayette, to whom a number of American towns had offered American nationality, returned to Versailles in triumph as the 'hero of two continents'. Received at the Petit Trianon, he danced a quadrille with Marie-Antoinette.

On 4 August 1785 there arrived at Versailles the 'American independence candelabra' commissioned by Louis XVI to commemorate the war: 'It is my honour to inform Monsieur le Directeur Général that in accordance with his orders I this morning had the candelabra of M. Thomire delivered to the King. His Majesty examined it attentively and appeared to view it with interest.'[21] This six-branched candelabra in gilt bronze on a marble pedestal, now on view in the King's Inner Cabinet at Versailles, was originally surmounted by a figurine of an Indian holding a bow in his right hand and a club in his left.

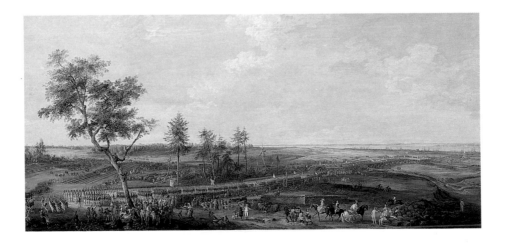

La Fayette
at Mount Vernon

In August 1784,
at the invitation of
George Washington,
whom he dubbed
'Patriarch of Liberty',
La Fayette stayed at
Mount Vernon. Although
he was invited back
on several occasions,
Washington by contrast
never visited France,
and was even to
become the architect
of American isolationism
at the time of the
revolutionary wars.

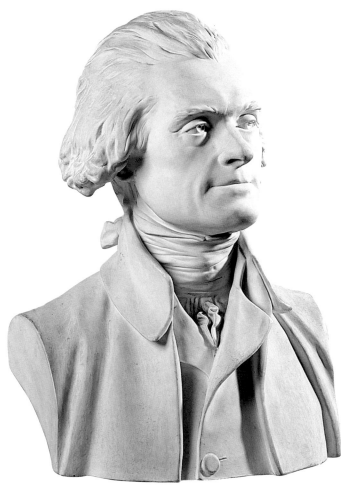

Thomas Jefferson

Minister plenipotentiary
of the United States
at the French court from
1785, Thomas Jefferson,
the sophisticated
and urbane Virginian
'aristocrat', was more at
ease at Versailles than
his predecessor Benjamin
Franklin had been.

France champions the United States

In the decorative arts of this period, the French monarchy and the American Revolution are closely linked, the American cap of liberty appearing frequently in association with the Bourbon fleur-de-lis, as on a medal entitled *Libertas Americana* and a *toile de Jouy* printed cotton of the same name, and in a set of Beauvais tapestries commissioned for the crown.

Thomas Jefferson, an American 'aristocrat' at Versailles

In 1785, La Fayette was reunited in Paris with his friend Thomas Jefferson, former governor of Virginia, who had been sent to France by the Americans in order to foster trade relations between the two countries. At the heart of these negotiations lay the famous Virginia tobacco, but oil from the white whales hunted by the deep-sea fishermen of Nantucket and New England also played a significant part. It was this oil, on which America was determined to retain its monopoly, that fueled the street lights of Paris and the thousands of lights that illumined Versailles during nocturnal entertainments.

The successor to Benjamin Franklin as American minister plenipotentiary in Paris, Thomas Jefferson was presented to the king on 14 May in an official ceremony of accreditation described at length by the Comte de Cheverny. Each ambassador climbed the Great Staircase at Versailles, on every step of which a Swiss Guard in dress uniform stood to attention. At the top, he was escorted to the King's State Bedchamber, where the high chamberlain and numerous other court dignitaries were in attendance. As the ambassador and his entourage were escorted into the room, the king rose and doffed his hat. The ambassador then bowed three times before His Majesty, who resumed his seat and covered his head once more. This was the sign for the ambassador to deliver his speech, taking care to doff his hat

'American homage to France'

At Jouy-en-Josas, only a short distance from Versailles, Christophe-Philippe Oberkampf produced cotton prints featuring subjects of topical interest, such as this example recalling the essential role of France in the War of Independence and making allusion to the necessity of free trade on the seas.

'American liberty'

In *Libertas Americana*, designed for the Jouy workshops in *c.*1784, Jean-Baptiste Huet celebrated the bucolic lifestyle of the colonists, and depicting sheep, cows, goats, hens, monkeys and butterflies living together in perfect harmony.

Commode and secretaire
of Marie-Antoinette

Commode and secretaire
in Japanese lacquer
and gilt bronze made by
the cabinetmaker Riesener
for Marie-Antoinette
at Versailles and
subsequently sent to
Saint-Cloud. One
of the finest ensembles
of furniture ever made in
France, it is now in
the Metropolitan Museum
of Art in New York.

each time he uttered the king's name. The king then spoke a few sentences in reply. Finally, the ambassador was presented to the queen and other members of the royal family.

Jefferson made a great impression at Versailles during these 'French years', if only because of the privileged position enjoyed by Americans in the wake of the special decree of 1778, by which the king granted their country the status of 'most-favored nation'.[22] And if Benjamin Franklin, so eager to be accepted by the French people, caused astonishment with his 'country squire' appearance, Jefferson, the son of a wealthy Virginia planter, was admired for his aristocratic bearing. At his elegant apartments in the Hôtel de Langeac in Paris he received his friends — who included not only La Fayette but also the Marquis de Chastellux who had fought in Rochambeau's army, Gouverneur Morris and the philosopher Condorcet — in gracious fashion, offering a distinguished table and exceptional wines. Nevertheless, he disliked the atmosphere at Versailles, and frequently complained of the tyrannical nature of court etiquette. When he later became President of the United States, he lost no time in abolishing protocol at his residence at Monticello.

The charge of 'Frenchification' which some of Jefferson's contemporaries levelled at him was after all a relative matter, for first and foremost he loved his own country and the flora and fauna of the great American open spaces, which he described in his *Notes sur la Virginie*, published on his arrival in France. These notes were the response to a 32-point questionnaire drawn up by the naturalist Georges Louis de Buffon, an exercise through which the government of Louis XVI hoped to become more familiar with the

American Independence candelabra

Commissioned from the famous bronzesmith Thomire to celebrate France's political victory over England, this candelabra was placed in the King's Inner Cabinet in 1785. It depicts a leopard symbolizing Britain vanquished by a Gallic cockerel.

Chaise à la reine by Foliot

One of a set
of four *à la reine* chairs
commissioned
in November 1780 from
François-Toussaint Foliot
for the Salon du Rocher
in the Queen's Hamlet
at the Petit Trianon.
The set is now in the
J. Paul Getty Museum
in Los Angeles.

Swivel chair by Jacob

In 1787, this armchair
was delivered
to Marie-Antoinette
for her Trelliswork
Bedchamber at the Petit
Trianon. It is now
in the J. Paul Getty
Museum in Los Angeles.

'America and Europe'

The covers of the
seats that accompanied
the Beauvais tapestries,
now in the Metropolitan
Museum of Art in New
York, featured traditional
images of America
— a land of plenty where
exotic and domestic
animals lived in harmony.

'America'

In 1786, Le Barbier
designed for the
Beauvais manufactory
cartoons for tapestries
depicting the four
corners of the globe.
In *America*, the traditional
figure of a young girl
in a feathered head-dress
was replaced by the
figure of liberty holding
aloft a star-spangled
banner.

American continent. With this same end in mind, in August 1785 Louis XVI sent Jean-François de Galaup, Comte de La Pérouse, on a scientific expedition to the Pacific. In his *Histoire Naturelle*, published from 1749 to 1804, Buffon accorded an important place to America, and owing to his influence, as Anne Vitart explains, 'the inhabitants of the New World and their possessions shed their status as curiosities and gradually assumed that of objects of scientific interest'.[23]

Thomas Jefferson was to remain in France until 1789, thus becoming a first-hand observer of the French Revolution, like his friend Gouverneur Morris. He was present at the meeting at Versailles of the Estates General, which made the great hall of the Hôtel des Menus Plaisirs their headquarters until the Third Estate decided to split off and meet alone in the Jeu de Paume, the real tennis court built under Louis XIV. Jefferson advised his friend La Fayette during the drawing up of the Declaration of the Rights of Man, inspired by the American Declaration of Independence, and he supported him in the wake of the storming of the Bastille on 14 July 1789, when La Fayette took command of the national guard. But in early October, when Jefferson was leaving for Le Havre where he was to embark for America, the mob invaded Versailles and threatened the safety of the royal family. La Fayette, for the moment defender of the monarchy once more, saved Marie-Antoinette. That day, Louis XVI and his family left the palace, never to return.

In his biography of Thomas Jefferson during his years in France, William Howard Adams concludes: 'For him [Jefferson], the French Revolution would become a sacred idea that transcended its individual leaders, including his closest friends.'

The Return

French officers returning from the United States, wreathed in glory, were greeted as heroes not only by their elders but also by the ladies of the court. In *The Return*, also known as *Double Recompense for Merit*, the painter Wille depicts a young man receiving from an older one not only the Cross of St Louis but also the hand of his daughter.

Versailles and America: from Louis XVI to Louis-Philippe

America and the French Revolution

On 21 January 1793, Louis XVI, the last absolute French monarch, was guillotined on the place de la Révolution in Paris. It was the sad conclusion to a precipitate series of events. Following his departure from Versailles in 1789, the king was kept under close guard in Paris. On 20 June 1791, he attempted to leave France with his family but was stopped at Varennes. On 10 August 1792, the mob attacked the Tuileries palace and the king and his family were taken prisoner. The monarchy was abolished and the Revolution became a bloodbath. The Commune was succeeded by the Terror under Robespierre, soon to be guillotined himself. In 1795, the Directoire was put in place, and four years later Napoleon Bonaparte took power, becoming Consul and finally Emperor of the French in 1804.

During the Revolution, Versailles was dismantled. Its art collections were sent to the Muséum, the Bibliothèque Nationale or the Conservatoire des Arts et Métiers. Its furniture was sold at public auction, where it was bought by numerous foreign connoisseurs, including Gouverneur Morris, who acquired the silk hangings and furniture from Marie-Antoinette's cabinet. The buildings were 'conserved and maintained at the expense of the Republic for the enjoyment of the people and to serve as establishments useful to agriculture and the Arts'. They became home to a natural history collection, a library, a music conservatoire and a gallery devoted to the French school of painting. Napoleon I, as emperor, dreamed once more of the magnificence of Versailles and imposed on his entourage a rigid court etiquette worthy of the Sun King himself. Moreover he frequently stayed at Trianon with the Empress Josephine and his family.

In America, on 22 April 1793, President George Washington delivered his famous speech on neutrality. The previous year, France had declared war

Louis-Philippe d'Orléans, Duc de Chartres

Of the numerous aristocrats from the court at Versailles who were obliged to flee France at the Revolution, many took refuge in the United States. These distinguished émigrés included not only the Marquise de la Tour du Pin and Talleyrand, but also a royal prince, Louis-Philippe d'Orléans, future King of the French, who made a lengthy stay in North America in 1796-8.

on Austria. Under the terms of the treaty signed at Versailles in 1778, the United States was required to lend France its support, but — in the first manifestation of American isolationism — Washington chose to defend America before the rest of the world. And while the Revolution had its sympathizers in the United States, notably among the followers of Jefferson, echoes of the Terror provided ammunition for its critics. Of the members of the French aristocracy who were forced to flee, some chose America as their place of exile. French émigrés gravitated towards the Huguenot communities established after the revocation of the Edict of Nantes, and small pockets of French culture began to appear.

In 1787 — aged just seventeen and decked out with diamonds lent to her by Marie-Antoinette herself — the Marquise de La Tour du Pin, *née* Dillon, was officially presented at court at Versailles. In 1795, we find this former lady-in-waiting to Marie-Antoinette farming an estate at Albany in Colonie County, on the west bank of the Hudson River. With her husband, once a colonel in the Royal-Vaisseaux regiment and now a farmer of fifty hectares of arable land, meadows, and orchards, she tended her kitchen garden and busied herself with making pats of butter bearing her coat-of-arms, which she sold in Albany market

On one occasion, Charles-Maurice de Talleyrand, Comte de Périgord and former bishop of Autun, surprised the lady in her farmyard, struggling valiantly to sever the bone of a leg of lamb. Her distinguished visitor — another member of that courtly aristocracy whose Versailles-centered universe had collapsed with the Revolution — gallantly exclaimed, 'Never has a leg of lamb been skewered in more majestic fashion!' Attracted by the potential of the United States, in 1794 Talleyrand too had decided to seek his

Antoine-Philippe
d'Orléans,
Duc de Montpensier

At the end of March 1797, Louis-Philippe and his two brothers, Antoine-Philippe d'Orléans, Duc de Montpensier, and Louis-Charles d'Orléans, Comte de Beaujolais, set off on a four-month voyage of discovery in the eastern states of America.

fortune there, through land speculation. At his new home in Philadelphia, where he had joined his fellow émigrés, the Vicomte de Noailles and the Duc de La Rochefoucauld-Liancourt, old friends from the days of Versailles, he was given to observing that he had 'found kindness' in the place of hatred and of 'all the folly and wickedness that possess our wretched Europe'.[24]

A French King

in the

United States

In New York State, meanwhile, Madame de Fériet, another former lady-in-waiting to Queen Marie-Antoinette, established the Hermitage, where she received a visit from Louis-Philippe, Duc d'Orléans, future King of the French, and his two brothers, the Duc de Montpensier and the Comte de Beaujolais. The express condition demanded by the revolutionary government for the release of the two latter — imprisoned in the Palais du Luxembourg in Paris and afterwards at Marseille — was that their elder brother should go into exile in America. Accordingly, on 24 September 1796, the Duc d'Orléans boarded the sailing ship *America* with his groom Beaudouin, to disembark twenty-seven days later in Philadelphia, then the largest city in the United States. Montpensier and Beaujolais joined him on 6 February 1797, after a grueling crossing lasting no less than ninety-three days. At the end of March, with the aid of funds advanced by Gouverneur Morris and dressed in leather trousers and cloth coats, they set off on horseback on a journey lasting almost four months and covering a broad itinerary. 'As they rode through Maryland, Virginia, the Alleghannies, Tennessee, the Cherokee Indian reservations and Kentucky, along the Ohio to Pittsburg, the lakes and Canada and back to Philadelphia from the north, they discovered cities in full expansion such as Baltimore and Washington, the federal capital, great barren expanses and dense forests, and made the

Souvenir du Mississippi

A sketch by the Duc de Montpensier, inspired by his highly picturesque travels in America with his brothers in 1797 and 1798.

acquaintance both of recent immigrants of all nationalities, seeking to make their fortune with greater or lesser success, and of the Indian peoples who were the first inhabitants of those lands.'[25]

This epic journey was not without its surprises. 'I must not overlook the events to which we were witness at the home of Captain Chapman,' wrote Louis-Philippe. 'There were only two beds in the bedchamber which formed the entire capacity of the house, and we were accorded merely "house room"; that is, we were given permission to spread our bedding on the uneven floorboards to both sides of the room, arranging our covers in such a way that we all four lay head on between the two beds with our feet by the fire. Captain Chapman got into one bed with his wife, which seemed to us most unaffected... He embarked upon a conversation with his wife of which we (though present) formed the subject, declaring that we were "strange fellows" to have left our home and endured all the fatigues of an arduous journey in order to see deserts, savages and a thousand other things that — not without some justice — he considered unworthy of our pains.'[26]

The royal threesome also took advantage of their journey to meet George Washington at Mount Vernon, and to visit the village of Tellico, where Louis-Philippe smoked a pipe of peace with the Indians and took his first steps in the Cherokee language. Brought up to respect the opposite sex, the future king was excessively shocked to discover that in these distant Indian lands, where life was governed by the laws of nature, the men set aside all the most difficult labors for the women, reserving the noblest tasks for themselves and devoting the best part of the day to smoking and leisurely conversation. The philosophical attitude of the royal travelers meanwhile aroused the wonder of some of the settlers, who marveled at the fact that

Panorama of Versailles

In 1814, the American artist John Vanderlyn painted one of the most interesting of all nineteenth-century panoramas, depicting the palace of Versailles and its gardens — although when it was put on display in New York from 1819 it did not enjoy the success he had hoped for. It is now in the Metropolitan Museum of Art in New York.

their financial difficulties had dampened neither their courage nor their spirits. After returning to Philadelphia, Louis-Philippe and his brothers set off on another journey, this time heading for Maine via Providence, New York, and Boston. From there, in late 1797, they travelled down the Ohio and Mississippi rivers to reach New Orleans. On 17 February 1798 they sailed for Havana, where they stayed for over a year and a half before returning to Europe via New York in January 1800.

Of all his memories of his youth, this American journey was always the one on which the king most enjoyed reminiscing in later life, never missing an opportunity to recall an incident or anecdote, especially on the occasions when he received with his customary kindness and courtesy American citizens who were traveling through France. The connection between America and the Orléans family was to prove an enduring one, for in 1861 and 1862 Louis-Philippe's two grandsons, the Comte de Paris and the Duc de Chartres, both crossed the Atlantic to fight in the Civil War.

An American painter at Versailles

In 1796, the same year that the Duc d'Orléans disembarked in America, another ship sailed the Atlantic to France, carrying among its passengers an American painter from Kingston in New York State: John Vanderlyn. In Paris, where he studied at the Academy with F.-A. Vincent, Vanderlyn became familiar with the new panoramas invented a few years earlier by a Scotsman, Robert Barker. This technique, which involved displaying long landscape paintings on the inner circular wall of a rotunda and lighting them from above in such a way as to give an illusion of perspective, became tremendously popular in French artistic circles, with rotundas being specially constructed for the purpose on boulevard Montmartre in 1799.

Vanderlyn's Panorama of Versailles

Under the Restauration, the popularity of Versailles remained undimmed, as may be seen in Vanderlyn's detailed painting.

At this point, Vanderlyn conceived the idea of painting a panorama of the palace of Versailles and its gardens, as he wrote to his brother: 'Here are a thousand statues at least of marble scattered about in groves, gardens, avenues and labyrinths which are formed of boskets and thickets and the beauty and grandeur I cannot describe, the imagination cannot conceive anything so inchanting, surrounded by so many gods and godesses though of marble that one expects nothing else but to see Nymphs sporting every minute.'[27] He started work in 1814, making numerous sketches before returning to America to complete the finished work. Back in New York, with the aid of several patrons he bought a plot of land close to City Hall and built a rotunda on the site. His panorama of Versailles, put on show there on 29 June 1819, received a generally enthusiastic welcome from the press, although some critics reproached Vanderlyn for not basing his work on a more universally familiar theme from American history. This singular work presented a picture of court life under Louis XVIII during the Restoration period, complete with a portrait of the king and some of his advisors at the balcony of one of the windows in the main wing of the palace. But its success was transitory, and above all it did not produce any substantial financial returns. Two years later, Vanderlyn took his panorama on a tour of the United States, exhibiting it notably in Philadelphia.

On 26 September 1852, he died at Kingston, crippled with debts and disillusioned by the indifferent reception of his work. Passed on to his descendants, the panorama was dismantled and for many years languished forgotten in a barn. In 1938, the Senate Association staged a retrospective of Vanderlyn's work, and in 1952 it presented the panorama to the Metropolitan Museum of Art in New York, where it is now on display.

Louis-Philippe and his sons

In 1837, Louis-Philippe, now King of the French, transformed the palace of Versailles into a 'Museum to all the glories of France', so saving from destruction a monument of great historical significance but which, for political reasons, could no longer serve as a royal palace. Here the king is depicted in front of the palace with his five sons.

Jefferson:

from Versailles

to Monticello

The lukewarm success of Vanderlyn's panorama is all the more surprising in view of the considerable strength of French influence at the time. In 1800, Thomas Jefferson, the 'most French of all Americans', was elected as president and installed the presidency in the new capital, Washington D.C., laid out by the French architect Pierre-Charles l'Enfant. From his years in Paris, Jefferson had brought back a number of foreign customs, to the surprise of visitors to Monticello, his residence at Charlottesville in Virginia. Taking his inspiration from the Hôtel de Salm, the architect-president decorated his house in French style. The rooms were furnished with pieces and paintings that he had collected in Paris, including a *Virgin Mary weeping over the Body of Christ* acquired at the auction of the property of Monsieur Billy, first valet to the king's wardrobe.[28] At his table, guests were offered menus of French inspiration prepared by his slave James Hemings, whom he had taken with him to France precisely so that he might learn the art of French cooking. Imported products such as French mustard added an authentic flavor, and the ices so prized by courtiers at Versailles now delighted guests in Virginia, one of whom, Daniel Webster, in 1824 observed that 'dinners at Monticello were served in half-Virginian, half-French style, in good taste and always abundance'.

French influence was also apparent in the design of the gardens at Monticello, created in 1779 and transformed in 1830 into a subtle combination of a park in English landscape style and gardens *à la française*, as noted by William Kelso: 'Consider the bounds of the rectangular leveled lawns, the rigorous symmetry of the garden platform, the straight row of houses on the straight Mulberry Row and the gridiron of trees and vineyard on the south slope.'[29] A plan of the gardens dated 1790 also

Cavelier de La Salle arriving in Louisiana

Any historical event in which French men or women played a prominent part was accorded its place in the new museum created by Louis-Philippe at Versailles, with a special emphasis surrounding those relating to the discovery and exploration of America. Hence Théodore Gudin was commissioned to paint a canvas depicting the arrival of Cavelier de La Salle on the coast of present-day Texas in January 1685.

mentions a 'bosquet of broom in the form of a spoked wheel'. At Versailles, six such bosquets punctuated the apparently straight lines of the *allées*.

North American examples of gardens in the style of Le Nôtre, which first made their appearance in the early part of the eighteenth century, included most notably Middleton Place in South Carolina, commissioned by Henry Middleton (1741); William Paca's garden in Annapolis (1760); the garden of William and Mary College in Williamsburg, Virginia (founded in 1693); Mount Vernon, residence of George Washington from 1754 to 1799; and finally the gardens of the Du Pont family in the state of Delaware.

At Wilmington, where Eleuthère Irénée Du Pont de Nemours (1771-1834), son of the French economist Pierre Samuel Du Pont de Nemours, settled after fleeing revolutionary France, the Nemours gardens may still be visited. Among their ornaments they boast 'marble sphinxes modeled after Louise de La Vallière',[30] originally from Colbert's château at Sceaux, and a rotunda sheltering a statue of Diana the huntress, cast by Jean-Antoine Houdon in 1780.

Though French influence remained strong, by the early nineteenth century the French colonial presence in the United States was a thing of the past. The most significant act of Jefferson's presidency was undoubtedly the purchase of Louisiana. Originally a French colony, this immense territory had later been subdivided on several occasions. In 1762, in gratitude for Spanish support during the Seven Years War against Britain, Louis XV had presented the lands to the west of the Mississippi to Spain. At the end of the war the following year, Britain inherited the lands to the east of the river, while France received the island of Santa Lucia in exchange. In 1798,

Louis XVI and
Benjamin Franklin
___

During the Restoration, the Sèvres manufactory, under the direction of Brongniart, created a large secretaire with a decorative scheme devoted to the history of Versailles. One of the porcelain plaques commemorates Louis XVI's reception of Benjamin Franklin at the palace in 1778.

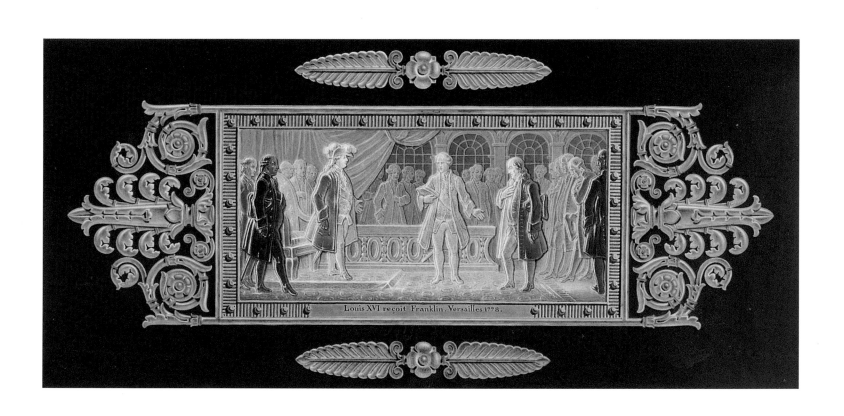

Louis XVI reçoit Franklin. Versailles 1778.

finally, after the end of the War of Independence and under the terms of the 1783 treaty, Spain recovered the whole of Louisiana, which it ceded to France once more in 1800. In 1802, Napoleon Bonaparte started to prepare an expedition to repopulate the territory, now French once again. Fearing lest this change of ownership should curtail free navigation of the Mississippi by American vessels, Thomas Jefferson dispatched a special envoy, Monroe, to negotiate with the French leader. At this point, the difficulties experienced by French settlers in Santo Domingo abruptly swung matters in the Americans' favor. Under the terms of an accord signed on 30 April 1803, the United States acquired a territory of 828,000 square miles for the sum of fifteen million dollars, thus striking the greatest land deal in history.

In a letter dated 18 July 1803, General Horatio Gates offered his congratulations to Jefferson: 'Let the land rejoice for you have bought Louisiana for a song.' With the acquisition of this great territory (afterwards subdivided into thirteen states), the United States doubled its size to become one of the largest — and soon one of the most powerful — of the world's nations. Preoccupied with his wars and the building of his great European empire, Napoleon thus allowed to slip through his fingers the 'French America' which at Versailles had been the stuff of Bourbon dreams.

First museum

of the New World

The final image of this New World that Versailles had so longed to conquer is provided by Louis-Philippe, Duc d'Orléans and erstwhile visitor to America, who became King of the French in August 1830. It was with a certain nostalgia that, on 21 April 1845, he received a delegation of Iowa Indians at the Tuileries. Their 'artistic director' (who would now be called

Louis XVI and the Comte de La Pérouse

Another porcelain plaque from the same secretaire shows Louis XVI with the navigator La Pérouse, sent to Hudson Bay by the king in 1782.

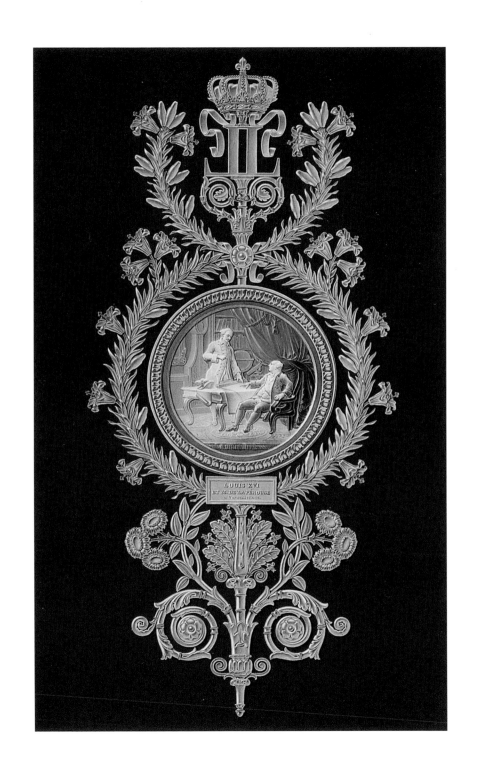

LOUIS XVI
ET M DE LA PEROUSE
A Versailles 1785.

an impresario) was the American painter George Catlin, who had traveled to England and afterwards France to present his collection of 600 paintings of the Indian way of life — then disappearing — in the hope of selling them to European governments. To add srength to his sales pitch, he had included in his trunks a variety of 'curiosities', which he exhibited with his paintings in an 'Indian gallery'.

In England, Catlin had encountered three groups of Iowa Indians who staged popular shows: 'They immediately chose the setting of my exhibition hall as the fitting place for their demonstrations with myself as the interpreter of their mysteries and amusements.'[31] The exoticism associated with the Amerindian world lingered on into the mid-nineteenth century, and as late as 1883 Mohawk Indians were exhibited behind bars in the botanical gardens in Paris. Thus it was that on 21 April in the Galerie de la Paix of the Tuileries Palace, before an audience including King Louis-Philippe, Queen Marie-Amélie and the Duchesse d'Orléans, a group of Iowa Indians performed 'their war dance and eagle dance to the sound of their own drum and war cries'. According to Catlin's own description, 'the savages wore their magnificent costumes of buffalo skins embroidered with porcupine quills and fringed with hair torn from their enemies' scalps. Their Majesties appeared to take great pleasure in this original and picturesque spectacle.'[32] One of the Indians presented the king with his tomahawk, his peace pipe and his whip, whereupon Louis-Philippe commissioned from Karl Girardet a painting depicting the scene and subsequently shown at the Salon in 1846. The king also bought fifteen copies of paintings from Catlin's Indian gallery to be put on show at the palace of Versailles, which he had recently returned to the French people.

Naval action
before Yorktown

For the new museum at Versailles Gudin was also commissioned to paint a canvas depicting the naval battle between the British Navy and the combined fleets of Admiral de Grasse and Barras de Saint Laurent, in Chesapeake Bay before Yorktown in 1781.

In 1837, Louis-Philippe had taken the decision to turn the palace into a museum dedicated to 'all the glories of France'. Five years of work funded personally by the king had resulted in the fitting out of 120 'historical galleries', in which were displayed six thousand paintings and two thousand sculptures exalting the grandeur of France and the heroic actions of great French men and women throughout history and across the globe. Through the initiative of the first French sovereign to have set foot on American soil, the principal events in the founding of the United States and the links that bind the two nations are thus commemorated at Versailles to this day. In *The Discovery of the St Lawrence by Jacques Cartier*, painted by Théodore Gudin in 1842, it is intriguing to note that the Indians depicted in the foreground are not members of the Micmac tribe encountered by the explorer in 1536, but rather Catlin's Iowa Indians, posed by their 'artistic director'. Two years later, Gudin was to follow this canvas with *The Discovery of Louisiana*. Louis-Philippe even went so far as to include a canvas depicting *The Capture of Yorktown*, painted by Couder in 1837, in the Galerie des Batailles, which was otherwise devoted exclusively to the celebration of glorious episodes from French history. Featured in the painting are the heroes of the War of Independence: Washington at the side of Rochambeau, with La Fayette behind him: 'Before the courage of the French a whole new drama opens up. The Americans have raised the standard of independence, Louis XVI sends a relief force to their aid; Rochambeau is in command; surrounded by young volunteers fired by the cause of liberty, he has the honor of fighting at the side of Washington and emerging victorious before Yorktown, and America is set free.'[33] To these military paintings commissioned from French artists, Louis-Philippe was to add a set of portraits of American

96

Victory at Yorktown

Without France, would America have won its independence? In the Galerie des Batailles, which chronicled glorious episodes in French military history, Louis-Philippe included the capture of Yorktown and the surrender of the British troops under General Cornwallis to George Washington.

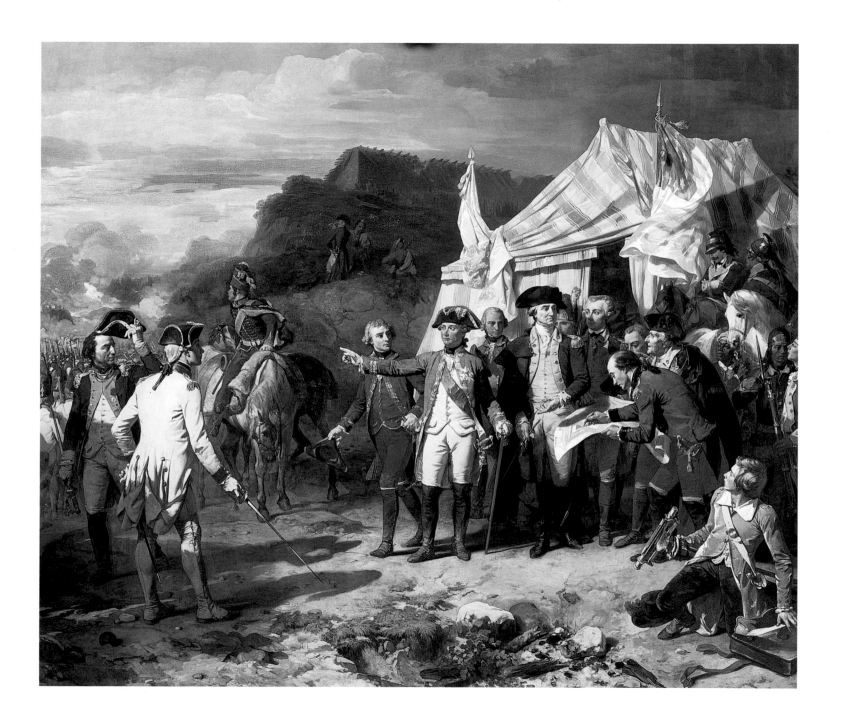

presidents, from George Washington to Andrew Jackson, painted by an American artist, George P. Healy (1808-94), introduced to the king in 1838. In addition to these canvases commissioned by Louis-Philippe, the collections at Versailles acquired a range of other paintings on American subjects. Some bear witness to the interest aroused in France by the American cause in the 1780s, such as *France presenting Liberty to America* by Jean Suau, which in 1784 won the prize of the Académie Royale in Toulouse under the title *The Great Revolution at Work in the New World*; the *Departure of La Fayette for the United States from the Spanish Port of Los Pasajes*, painted by Hubert Robert; and *The Signature of the Declaration of American Independence by John Hancock* painted by George P. Healy. The *Portrait of George Washington victorious at the Battle of Princeton* by Charles Wilson Peale, meanwhile, was a gift from the United States government. Some of these works are still at Versailles, either on display or in the reserve collections, while others have been transferred to the Musée National de la Coopération Franco-Américaine at Blérancourt.

America's part in the new museum created by Louis-Philippe was one of some prominence, reflecting the importance invested in the New World by Versailles under the Ancien Régime. It was from Versailles, after all, that explorers and colonists had set off to conquer this new continent, and it was Versailles that had helped the American nation to attain its ideal. It was the descendants of Rochambeau and La Fayette, members of the Order of Cincinnati and of the Sons of the American Revolution, who in 1875 were to finance the subscription for the construction of the Statue of Liberty presented to the United States on 28 October 1886.

Reception of
Iowa Indians
by Louis-Philippe

Louis-Philippe treasured fond memories of his time in the United States. At the Tuileries in 1845, he received a delegation of Iowa Indians who 'performed their war dance and eagle dance to the sound of their own drum and war cries'.

II

Versailles and America
in
the twentieth century

The United States and Versailles

The Société des

Amis

de Versailles

It was in 1913 that Woodrow Wilson was elected twenty-eighth president of a United States which, since the annexation of Hawaii, had assumed its definitive boundaries and counted some hundred million inhabitants. With the development of industry, great fortunes had been amassed: J. Pierpont Morgan, who died in 1913, founded the first great capitalist bank; Henry Ford had applied the techniques of mass production to automobiles; and John Davison Rockefeller, owner of Standard Oil, had become the world's first oil magnate. Also in 1913, he created the Rockefeller Foundation, 'to improve the wellbeing of humanity in the world' (the culmination of a philanthropic achievement which had begun in 1889 with the funding of the University of Chicago). On the eve of the First World War, New York had forged a reputation as a capital of the arts, with the first exhibition of American painting at the Armory Show in that same year. This was a youthful democracy that had already outgrown the European model of bloody revolutions.

Just as peace in Europe was now on the brink of collapse, so was the fabric of Versailles. With the memory of the restoration campaigns undertaken by Louis-Philippe now fading, the roof had started to leak, while the French state, preoccupied on other fronts, took no action.

It was a journalist on the *Echo de Paris*, Eugène Tardieu, who sounded the alarm bell in 1907. Of the dilapidated state of the Petit Trianon he observed: 'there are no longer any windows left, the collapsed thatched roofs let the rain in… By night, ruffians and vagabonds meet in the cottages which provide convenient and undisturbed shelter (there are three guards to patrol 92 hectares!). Happily they confine themselves to sleeping and depositing their filth there…'

The Treaty of Versailles

Alongside the signatures of the British delegation are those of their American counterparts including Woodrow Wilson, the first president of the United States to leave American soil, in defiance of the views of his advisors.

The signature
of the Treaty of Versailles

In 1783, the treaty
establishing American
independence had
been signed at Versailles;
now, on 28 June 1919,
another Treaty, signed in
the Hall of Mirrors
at Versailles, marked the
beginning of a new era.

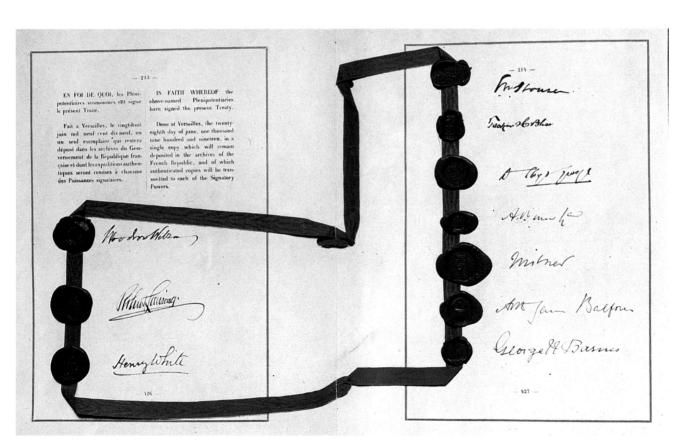

This shocking catalogue finally roused public opinion. Distinguished personalities from the world of the arts joined forces to found the Société des Amis de Versailles: founder members included Victorien Sardou, author of *Madame Sans-Gêne*, and the painters Léon Bonnat and Edouard Detaille, with Alexandre Millerand, later President of the Republic, as president. Georges Berger, parliamentary deputy for Paris and president of the Union Centrale des Arts Décoratifs and the Société des Amis du Louvre, offered the new society premises in the Pavillon de Marsan in the Louvre, which it occupied until its return to Versailles in 1980. In 1913, on the initiative of the Société des Amis du Louvre and the Société des Amis du Luxembourg, the Société des Amis de Versailles received official recognition from the state.

The Treaty of Versailles

In August 1914, Europe descended into war. In the U.S. Congress, Woodrow Wilson was initially at pains to emphasize American neutrality; but with the development of submarine warfare, led by the Germans, and the sinking of the *Lusitania* on 9 May 1915, America was inexorably drawn into the conflict. On 6 April 1917, Congress declared war on Germany. Two million American troops were shipped across the Atlantic, under the supreme command of General Pershing — of whom a full-length portrait by Cecilia Wentworth may now be seen at Versailles. Since April 1917, meetings of a military council of the joint Allied forces had been held at the Trianon Palace Hotel at Versailles, built in 1910 by the architect René Sergent. America's entry into the war, in which 53,000 American troops were to die at the front, radically changed the balance of power within the Allied forces. The U.S. banks, including most notably the Morgan Bank, helped to

The Hall of American Independence

In order to reaffirm the unbreakable ties between France and the United States, in 1919 a 'Hall of American Independence' was inaugurated at Versailles. Assembled here, on the initiative of Pierre de Nolhac, were busts, portraits, and paintings associated with the War of Independence.

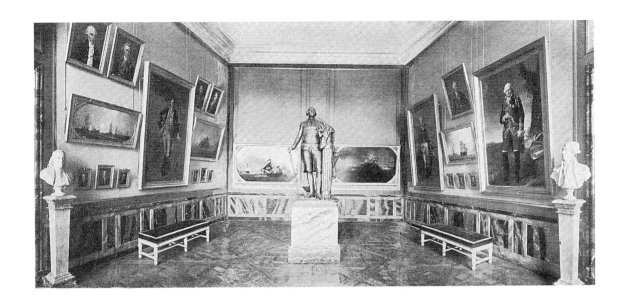

General Pershing

The museum
at Versailles houses
this portrait of
American General
John Joseph Pershing,
Commander-in-Chief
of the U.S. army
who was present in
France during
the First World War.

fund the war effort with loans of ten billion dollars. Encircled at last, Germany surrendered; on 11 November 1918, the signing of the Armistice signaled the end to this terrible war.

While the other victors proposed that the Peace Conference that followed should be held in Geneva, America was not in agreement. It was at this juncture that Georges Clemenceau, the French Prime Minister, suggested Versailles as the venue. *The Times* was eloquent in its support of the idea, insisting that financial concerns were not the only criterion, and that moral and symbolic factors should also be taken into account in the selection of an appropriate venue for the signature of the peace accord. By carrying out the negotiations in France, the Allies would be paying due tribute to the suffering and heroism of the French people. The French army, fighting alongside American soldiers on the tragic battlefield of Sedan, had already begun to wash away the stain of the crushing French defeat by Prussia on that same spot in 1870. The signature of the peace accord in the Hall of Mirrors at Versailles, where the now vanquished German Empire had been proclaimed with such solemnity in 1871, would at last put the final touches to the most symbolic peace process in the history of Europe. American feeling was wholly in favor of this idea. It was also at Versailles that the treaty establishing American independence had been signed in 1783.[34]

On 18 November 1918, against the advice of those who insisted that no American president had ever left the shores of the United States while in office, Wilson announced that he would be present at the Peace Conference in person. On 13 December, the president with many advisors steamed into the port of Brest aboard the *George Washington*, escorted by battleships and

Inauguration of the monument to General Pershing

On 6 October 1937, Albert Lebrun, President of the French Republic, inaugurated the Versailles memorial in the presence of General Pershing, Marshal Pétain, numerous other prominent figures and three thousand veterans of the American Legion.

**Design for the monument
to General Pershing**

In 1937 the town
of Versailles, vaunting
itself proudly as
the cradle of American
independence,
launched a national
subscription to raise
a monument to the glory
of the American army
and of General Pershing.

destroyers of the French and American navies. From there, they were taken by the French presidential train to Paris, cheered all the way by crowds applauding Wilson as the hero of the peace. In Paris he stayed with his wife at the Hôtel du Prince Murat, while the American delegation occupied the Hôtel Crillon. On 18 January 1919, the first session of the conference was officially opened at Versailles, a momentous scene witnessed by the American Warwick Greene: 'Yesterday Versailles shone in its best glory. It was designed as a stage for great events, not for tourists to gape at, and yesterday was an event to its liking. True, it looked down contemptuously, from its regal and colorful beauty, on the frog coats and tall hats ... of our statesmen who seemed more than ever like white-faced crows ... stalking about amid splendors which had once known statesmen in harmony with the surroundings and park.'[35] Georges Clemenceau, dubbed 'The Tiger', presided over the session, with the American president seated on his right. On 8 January Woodrow Wilson, a supporter of multilateral diplomacy, had expounded in Congress the 'fourteen points' anticipating the Society of Nations, which were to serve as a basis for the negotiations.

It was to take spokesmen for the Allies no less than six months to convince the German delegation, led by Count Bockdorff Rantzau, but at last, on 28 June 1919, the ceremonial signing of the Treaty of Versailles took place in the Hall of Mirrors. Georges Clemenceau, 'Father of the Victory', had invited representatives of wounded ex-servicemen — 'breathing gargoyles', in Warwick Greene's description — to be present at this historic occasion. 'No ornament of any kind. No embellishment or decorum. The atmosphere of the signing of a legal document,' observed one witness. 'The sole furniture was a long horseshoe-shaped table at which sat the Allied delegates and

Elsie de Wolfe

The first American interior decorator and a passionate devotee of the French *art de vivre*, Elsie de Wolfe — Lady Mendl — made her home at the Villa Trianon at Versailles in 1907.

Anne Morgan

Numerous American personalities came to the aid of France during the First World War. Anne Morgan, daughter of J. P. Morgan, set up an ambulance service at Versailles for wounded servicemen. In 1927, she donated her château at Blérancourt to the French state to house the Musée de la Coopération Franco-Américaine.

their associates, each with their ink blotter, their penholder and their cut-glass inkwell arranged in front of them. No chandeliers. No consoles or *guéridons* that might distract the attention. Around the long horseshoe-shaped table, other tables and two hundred chairs supplied by the Mobilier National were arranged on twenty-four Savonnerie carpets. Opposite the centre table stood an elegant Louis XV desk, with an armchair in the same style beside it. On the desk, a Louis XIV inkwell. Here the master of ceremonies, M. de Fouquières, placed a large volume which he took from a white case: the Treaty of Versailles.'[36] The representatives of the twenty-seven Allied nations and of Germany then put their signatures to the final accord.

After the ceremony, which lasted a little under an hour, Georges Clemenceau, Woodrow Wilson and Lloyd George, all wearing top hats, stood on the steps outside. Cameras flashed. A cannon roared. Behind the palace railings, a crowd had gathered to glimpse the dignitaries who had just sealed their future. 'If the splendid dead could rise, millions and millions of them, how they would have thronged those radiant summer skies above Versailles!'[37]

The Salon bleu
at the Villa Trianon

At the Villa Trianon,
Elsie de Wolfe received
numerous American
expatriates including
Anne Morgan,
Anna Gould and
the painter Walter Gay.
This painting is one
of a number of interiors
done for her by Gay.

Versailles conquers America

The delegates invited to the talks at Versailles could not help but be struck by the excessively dilapidated condition of the palace buildings. And yet the Société des Amis de Versailles remained on the alert. As the current president, the Vicomte de Rohan, observed in 1999: 'In accordance with the spirit of its founders, the members of the Société des Amis de Versailles are the palace's vestal virgins. They maintain that essential contact with the public without which the renovation, the embellishment and the enrichment of

The Villa Trianon
at Versailles

Elsie de Wolfe
restored the Villa
Trianon with
the advice of Pierre
de Nolhac, chief
curator of the
palace of Versailles.

Versailles would be impossible. For we must constantly demonstrate to the powers that be that Versailles is loved and visited.' Thus the society's efforts in those early days were in the end to bear fruit.

A law passed on 23 December 1923 set in place a state loan of one and a half million francs over a period of five years, to be devoted to the buildings' structure and their maintenance on a regular basis. To supplement this source of income, the society raised funds privately through seasons of cultural events. It also cultivated relations with collectors, most notably in the United States, with a view to helping the palace curators to refurnish rooms that had lain empty since the Revolution. In this respect, the affair of the Sèvres Marshals' table set an interesting precedent. Put up for auction, this celebrated piece commissioned by Napoleon was bought by 'Monsieur Guillaume Hearst, monopoly-owner of American newspapers' for the sum of four hundred thousand francs. At this point, the curator of the Musée de la Malmaison (Napoleon's favourite residence) intervened to invoke a law voted in on 31 December 1923, which accorded the state a right of preemption on 'objects forming part of France's historic heritage'. Lacking sufficient funds to buy back the table, even with state aid, the curator put the matter in the hands of another American, Edward Tuck. As the Paris correspondent of the *New Yorker*, Janet Flanner, observed somewhat drily: 'In order to prevent the rich American Mr. Hearst from having the Marshals' table, the rich American Mr. Tuck known and beloved here for his many princely restorations to France of her own property, paid the price.'[38]

Fortunately for Versailles, France was very much in vogue in America between the wars. The children of fashionable New England families were taught French at home and were frequently sent to complete their studies

Interior of
the Petit Trianon

Having settled in France with his wife, the American artist Walter Gay specialized in painting the most elegant interiors of the period, public and private, including not only the Petit Trianon but also the Ganay residence at Courances and Saint-Georges-Motel, home of Mme Jacques Balsan, *née* Vanderbilt.

at the Sorbonne. Paris was *the* place to be. The Surrealists could be found dining at the Deux Magots café in Saint Germain; Josephine Baker, clad only in a single pink flamingo feather, sang in the *Revue Nègre*; in cabarets couples danced the foxtrot, imported from the United States, and nightlife carried on into the small hours in the clubs of the Champs-Elysées. Sylvia Beach published James Joyce's *Ulysses* in Paris in 1922, and Isadora Duncan danced there for the last time. The expatriate American community was glittering — at one of Anna de Noailles' *soirées*, for instance, one might run across Edith Wharton, author of *The House of Mirth*, who had lived in France since 1913 — and above all glamorous. A cosmopolitan crowd rushed elegantly from one extravagant party to the next: a fancy dress party at Elsa Maxwell's, where everyone had to dress up 'like someone everybody knew — at least by sight', or an oriental evening staged by the Americans' favorite couturier (and rival in pre-eminence of Gabrielle 'Coco' Chanel), Paul Poiret. And everyone who loved Paris also had a soft spot for Versailles, whose sophisticated brand of elegance had inspired the first professional American interior decorator, Elsie de Wolfe — Lady Mendl. Since 1907, Elsie de Wolfe had made her home in the Villa Trianon at 47 boulevard Saint-Antoine, a haven of peace not far from the palace. With the advice of Pierre de Nolhac, then curator of Versailles, she embarked on a historically accurate restoration not only of the villa but also of its gardens and a cottage built for Marie-Antoinette's physician in the style of the Queen's Hamlet. Here this fervent admirer of Louis XIV received Anne Morgan, Boni de Castellane and Anna Gould,[39] who had used part of her American fortune to build the Palais Rose, inspired by the Grand Trianon, on avenue Foch in the fashionable heart of Paris.

The Pavillon de la Lanterne at Versailles

The American press baron Gordon Bennett lived in the Pavillon de la Lanterne in the early 1900s. The U.S. ambassador, the Honorable David Bruce, and his wife Evangeline were also resident there immediately after the Second World War. Nowadays, the Pavilion is at the disposal of the French Prime Minister.

The entrance to the
Pavillon de la Lanterne

The stags' heads
flanking the gates
to the pavilion
came originally from
Louis XIV's
Menagerie nearby.

On the other side of the Atlantic, Versailles remained an equally inexhaustible source of inspiration. Taking their lead from Ludwig II of Bavaria, who erected a replica of the central wing of the palace on his island of Herrenchiemsee, from the late nineteenth century American millionaires built residences such as Bellefontaine, a replica of the Petit Trianon, created in 1899 at Lennox in the Berkshires by the architects Carrère and Hastings. In 1896, Frederick William Vanderbilt (1856-1938), grandson of the railway magnate Cornelius Vanderbilt (1794-1877), built a 55-room residence at Hyde Park on the banks of the Hudson River. He entrusted the design of this large mansion to the Manhattan architects McKim, Mead and White, famous for their Beaux Arts buildings; the interior decorations, meanwhile, by the architect Ogden Codman, included a bedroom in the Louis XV style for Mrs. Vanderbilt, complete with a bed screened by a balustrade, as in the Queen's Bedchamber at Versailles.

From 1916 to 1920, at Chestnut Hill in Pennsylvania, the banker Edward Townsend Stotesbury (1849-1938), owner of Drexel & Company, erected Whitemarsh Hall, a veritable royal palace, visited by the French statesman Georges Clemenceau on his tour of the United States in 1922: 'One day Clemenceau… looked down the mile-long vista that sloped gently away from the terraced classical gardens of the palace and was reminded of Versailles, perhaps with a certain rue.'[40] There was even a rotunda sheltering statues of female figures draped in antique style, similar to those positioned by Madame du Barry for Louis XV's visit to Louveciennes in 1771. In 1918, Hubert Templeton Parson, president of Woolworth, bought the Shadow Lawn estate in New Jersey, only to have it transformed — by the architect Horace Trumbauer and the French landscape designer Achille

Louis XVI's library
at Versailles

In her book
The Decoration of Houses,
published in 1897,
the distinguished
writer and passionate
francophile
Edith Wharton took
Louis XVI's library
as her model.
On her death in 1937,
she was buried in the
cemetery of Les Gonards
at Versailles, alongside
American soldiers
who had fallen during
the First World War.

Dining room at
Marble House,
Newport, Rhode Island

The dining room at
Marble House, paneled
throughout in colored
marble, was inspired by
the Hercules Salon at
Versailles.
On the chimneypiece
— a replica of the one at
Versailles — hangs a
portrait of the Sun King,
of whom Alva Vanderbilt
was said to be a fervent
admirer.

Duchêne — in a style betraying the unmistakable influence of Versailles, including such features as the Ionic columns of the central wing overlooking the gardens and the balustrade from the Petit Trianon. As James T. Maher observed in *The Twilight of Splendor*, 'at Shadow Lawn, Trumbauer was serving monarchic pretensions'. The harmonious elevations with their restrained decoration were also reminiscent of the Petit Trianon: 'It is not only the size of the palace that astonishes the eye: one is also immediately impressed by the severity of the south façade. ...The hand of the designer at Shadow Lawn is restrained by Gabriel — the straight line contains any impulse to fugal wanderings.'[41] In the formal gardens laid out to the west of the palace by Achille Duchêne, 'the colonnades he used to close the north and west sides of the formal gardens… were adapted from the circular peristyle known as "la Colonnade" [laid out by Jules Hardouin-Mansart in 1685] in the *bosquet* at Versailles.'

The gardens of Le Nôtre found another echo in Longwood Gardens in Pennsylvania, the property of Pierre Du Pont (1870-1954), descendant of the great family of industrialists. The same classical influence may also be seen at work in the gardens of Dumbarton Oaks in the Georgetown area of Washington, designed by Edith Wharton's niece Beatrix Farrand for the diplomat Robert Bliss (1875-1962) and his wife Mildred.

The French Pavilion at the 1904 World Fair, Saint Louis, Missouri

Bearing witness once again to the almost mythical power of the image of Versailles in America, the French Pavilion for the World Fair at Saint Louis, Missouri in 1904 was a replica of the Grand Trianon. It housed an exhibition of Sèvres porcelain and Beauvais and Gobelins tapestries on themes associated with Louis XIV.

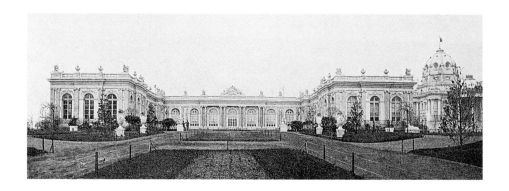

Marble House,
Newport, Rhode Island

At Newport, American
families vied with each
other in the construction
of seaside villas inspired
by European palaces.
Marble House, built for
Mr. and Mrs. William K.
Vanderbilt by the
architect Richard Morris
Hunt in 1888-92,
owes its inspiration to
the Petit Trianon.

Rosecliff,
Newport, Rhode Island

Not far from Marble
House stood Rosecliff,
built in 1901 for Mr. and
Mrs. Hermann Oelrichs.
Here the architect
Stanford White adopted
the U-shaped plan of the
Grand Trianon, glazing
the colonnade linking the
two wings of the building
— and thus giving it the
appearance of the palace
in the nineteenth century.

**Burden Mansion,
New York**

While William K. and
Alva Vanderbilt took
their inspiration for
their residence on Fifth
Avenue in New York
from the châteaux of the
Loire, James A. Burden
preferred the classical
style for his mansion on
91st Street, built between
1902 and 1905 by
the architect Whitney
Warren. One of
the drawing rooms is an
interpretation of the
marble-lined interiors at
Versailles.

Monsieur Beaucaire

The dream of Versailles
also inspired the
great American movie
directors. In 1924,
Sidney Olcott made
Monsieur Beaucaire,
a screen adaptation of
a novel by the American
writer Mrs. Booth
Tarkington. The drama,
starring Rudolph
Valentino, was filmed
entirely in the studios, on
sets reproducing the park
and palace of Versailles.

Marie-Antoinette

While the restoration
work undertaken
at Versailles focused
international attention
on the palace, the luxury
and intrigues of the
French court provided
the seductive background
for a number of
Hollywood spectaculars.
In 1938, Norma Shearer
as Marie-Antoinette
was courted by Tyrone
Power as Fersen in
Marie-Antoinette, directed
by Woody S. Van Dyke.

John Davison

Rockefeller Jr.

patron

of Versailles

In 1923, Maurice Paléologue, historian, ambassador, president of the Société des Amis de Versailles and of the Rockefeller donations committee, organized a private visit to Versailles for the heir to the Standard Oil empire, John D. Rockefeller Jr. (1874-1960). Following in his father's philanthropic footsteps, the younger Rockefeller declared a particular interest in the cultural heritage of humanity. Versailles, with all its wealth of symbolic associations, could not leave him unmoved — especially in the wake of the First World War, which had strengthened the bonds of friendship between France and America. 'The First World War became the event which made France popular in American eyes,' explains Françoise Ouzan, 'for their newspapers carried reports of the shelling and destruction. The war enabled them to discover a country of which they had until that point fostered a fairly hazy image.'[42]

America had flown to the aid of France in her hour of need, just as France had once extended a helping hand across the Atlantic. Through committees and voluntary associations the French people had received aid from numerous American individuals, such as Anne Morgan, who in 1927 donated her château at Blérancourt to the nation. Versailles benefited greatly from this surge of generosity. Following his visit, John D. Rockefeller Jr. wrote to the French Prime Minister Raymond Poincaré: 'Returning to France last summer after an interval of seventeen years, I was impressed anew with the beauty of her art, the magnificence of her architecture, and the splendors of her parks and gardens. Many examples of these are not only national but international treasures, for which France is trustee; their influence on the art of the world will always be full of inspiration. ...I should count it a privilege to be allowed to help toward [their restoration], and shall be happy

Restoration work
at Versailles
betweeen the wars

The very considerable sums generously donated by John D. Rockfeller Jr. from 1923 enabled restoration work to be carried out not only on the palace roofs but also on the buildings and waterfeatures of the park.

The Mill in the Queen's
Hamlet in the 1920s

Already restored
once under the Empire
in the early nineteenth
century, by the end
of the First World War
the Queen's Hamlet at
Trianon was again
on the verge of collapse.

The Mill at Trianon
during restoration

The restoration carried
out in the 1920s
involved consolidating
all the walls, relaying
the thatched roofs from
scratch and re-creating
the cottage gardens.

Restoration of one
of the *pièces d'eau*
on the North Parterre

The restoration work
funded by John D.
Rockefeller Jr. started
in 1924, under
the direction of the chief
architect to the palace
Patrice Bonnet.

to contribute one million dollars, its expenditure to be entrusted to a small committee composed of Frenchmen and Americans ... this money should be used for the reconstruction of the roof of Rheims Cathedral; for the reconditioning of the buildings, fountains and gardens of Versailles; and for the purpose of making repairs that are urgently needed in the palace and gardens of Fontainebleau.'[43]

The Franco-American committee, with Rockefeller's architect Welles Bosworth as its secretary, was lent premises in the offices of the Ministry of Culture in Paris. With successive donations in 1923, 1927 and 1932, (23 million dollars in all) Rockefeller thus funded the restoration of the roofs of the palace, the Petit Trianon and the Queen's Hamlet, and of the pools and statues in the park. For twelve years, from his office in New York or his country house on the banks of the Hudson River, he followed the progress of these works step by step. Finally, on 30 June 1936, 'the magnificent contribution of a citizen of the United States' was celebrated in suitably imposing fashion. 'Building had always been Junior's overriding passion. All his favorite works — Williamsburg, The Cloisters [presented by him to the Metropolitan Museum in 1938], Versailles — were highly elaborate constructions. With these he could observe and measure the day-to-day progress of the work accomplished.'[44]

The Bosquet des
Rocailles
during restoration
_____

The restoration of this
bosquet (Salle de bal)
involved dismantling the
dilapidated seventeenth-
century structure.

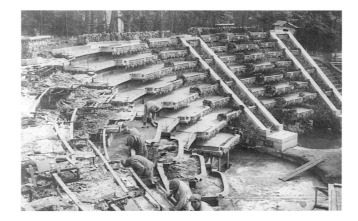

The Bosquet des
Rocailles
after restoration
_____

In this bosquet, all the
rockwork was rebuilt,
the urns and large
tripods were restored
and regilded, and
the canalization of the
fountains completely
refurbished.

Inauguration of the
restored Bosquet des
Rocailles.
_____

On 30 June 1936,
John D. Rockefeller Jr.
and his wife were received
with great ceremony
at Versailles, where the
fountains in the
Bosquet des Rocailles
now played once more
as they did in the
seventeenth century.

Small arm of
the Grand Canal
———————————

These photographs
reveal not only
the lamentable state
of the park at Versailles
in certain places but also
the herculean scale of
the restoration work
necessary, as witnessed
in 1936 by John D.
Rockefeller Jr., seen
here with the Director
of the Beaux-Arts.

Unveiling of the plaque
in honor of
John D. Rockefeller Jr.

———

A plaque in the
Vestibule Gabriel
at the Museum
of Versailles expresses
the gratitude of the
French people to
the great American
philanthropist and
patron of the arts, who
declared: 'What I must
do is not what other
people can do, it's what
other people can't do.'

The United States supports the Museum of Versailles

**Versailles
and American
patronage
after the Second
World War**

As the Second World War finally dragged to a close on all fronts, with the formal surrender of Japan on 2 September 1945, France was left weak and drained. Once again, American troops had disembarked in France in order to bolster the Allied defence against Germany. Meanwhile, Harry S. Truman had succeeded Franklin D. Roosevelt (who had died on 12 April 1945) as president of a United States which was about to embark on a period of unparalleled prosperity: 'in 1948, over three-quarters of the world's automobiles were American'. New York, now the world's chief capital city, became in addition the seat of the United Nations, thanks to a gift from John D. Rockefeller Jr. of 8.5 million dollars for the site of the organization's headquarters on the banks of the East River. With the revolution brought about by Jackson Pollock and Marc Rothko, New York also established itself as a leader of the avant-garde in art, while still remaining attached to the aesthetic of the Old World — Christian Dior's 'New Look', for example, was a wild success in the United States.

In 1946, a new deputy curator, Gerald Van der Kemp, was appointed to Versailles: a gesture of gratitude from the French government to the man who, as wartime head of stores at the château of Valençais, had been responsible for saving the *Venus de Milo*, the *Winged Victory of Samothrace* and many other works of art from being pillaged by the German forces. He was to find Versailles in a parlous state, as he himself recounted: 'The situation was disastrous when I arrived. Everything had suffered. To start with, there had been no heating for five years. Then the furniture had been dispersed. The large paintings that remained, such as those in the Galerie des Batailles, were bleached and covered in mould. The varnish had frozen. ...

Le Bosquet de la Colonnade

In 1948, the gift by Mrs. S.D. Bliss of twenty paintings depicting the bosquets at Versailles was the first of a new series of generous donations by American citizens.

Marie-Antoinette's Bedchamber

The weaving of replicas of the remarkable silks that originally decorated the queen's bedchamber was made possible in 1953 by an exceptional donation from the Kress Foundation.

In addition, the condition of Trianon was alarming.'[45] The French government granted the palace a loan of one million francs over five years to deal with the most pressing matters. But the buildings seemed tragically empty. In a first symbolic gesture, the new curator had all the palace's 200 clocks rewound, before setting himself the ambitious target of refurnishing the interior throughout. Originally, the 2500 rooms of the palace, forming 288 suites of apartments, were occupied by 5000 inhabitants, who also enjoyed the use of a 1200-seat theater and 850 hectares of gardens, embellished with 1400 fountains and maintained by an army of 2000 gardeners.

Versailles owed its international reputation not only to the beauty of its architecture and gardens, but also to the fascination exercised by the nature of court life — glittering and sumptuous — under Louis XIV, Louis XV and Louis XVI. The original splendor of the palace might have vanished forever, but Gerald Van der Kemp hoped nevertheless to evoke something of its former magnificence for visitors of today. To realize this dream, he naturally turned to the country to which his Dutch ancestors had emigrated, and which had bestowed such generosity on France since the First World War.

Van der Kemp's elegance and sense of humor were appreciated as much in the States as they were in France, and his friends, including David Rockefeller, Louise de Vilmorin and Nancy Mitford, author of *The Sun King*, were only too happy to lend their support. Tokens of friendship and loyalty were soon flooding in: in 1948 Mrs. S.D. Bliss presented a set of twenty oil paintings depicting details from the gardens at Versailles (bosquets, fountains, and portiques) which now hang in the château and the Grand Trianon. The following year, Barbara Hutton (1912-79), granddaughter of

Sèvres porcelain plaque

In 1954, Rushmore Kress, heir to the Kress Foundation, presented the museum with two cabinets in *bois d'amboine* with Sèvres porcelain plaques originally in the possession of Queen Hortense.

the founder of the Woolworth empire who had married Prince Trubetskoy, restored the original Savonnerie carpet, made in the mid-eighteenth century for Queen Maria Leszczynska, to the Queen's State Bedchamber.

But in 1953 tragedy struck, when the chief curator of Versailles, Louis Mauricheau-Beaupré, was killed in a flying accident during a long fund-raising tour of America. He was succeeded by Gerald Van der Kemp. A prolific figurative painter, Van der Kemp had no hesitation in traveling to America the following year to sell his own canvases in order to finance trips to Washington, Philadelphia, Cleveland, Chicago, and Palm Beach. That same year, his efforts were rewarded by a major donation from the Kress Foundation, a philanthropic organization founded in 1929 by S.H. Kress, pioneer of mass distribution. With this gift, work could start on the restoration of Marie-Antoinette's bedchamber. Rushmore Kress, heir to the foundation, also presented the palace with 'two cabinets in *bois d'amboine*, decorated with Sèvres porcelain plaques' and now on display in the former Queen's Billiard Room. In 1954, the five sons of John D. Rockefeller Jr. — Laurance, David, Winthrop, Nelson, and John D. III — completed the work of restoration started by their father at Trianon and the Queen's Hamlet. In October 1955, a lady from New York donated a 'clock in turned ivory and silvered bronze' dating from the eighteenth century and probably originally from the château of Bellevue. A year later, a donation from ambassador Douglas Dillon enabled the American Friends of Versailles, forerunner of the Versailles Foundation, to purchase two Riesener corner cabinets from the Louis XVI Games Room, while Marjorie Merriweather-Post, wife of the first US ambassador to the Soviet Union, made a gift of four paintings by Jean-Baptiste Oudry.

Ambassador Dillon at Versailles

Ambassador Dillon, his wife and daughter H.R.H. Princess Charles de Luxembourg, pictured in front of the palace with Gerald Van der Kemp, chief curator from 1953 and the moving force behind the refurnishing of Versailles.

Corner cabinet from the Louis XVI Games Room

Thanks to the generosity of Douglas Dillon, United States ambassador to France from 1953 to 1957, the Louis XVI Games Room has now recovered a pair of corner cabinets originally delivered to the palace in 1774 by the cabinetmaker Riesener.

In 1957, an anonymous donation to the American Friends of Versailles bought a six-legged console table in carved wood with a marble top, dating from the reign of Louis XVI and now on display in the Apollo Salon. Barbara Hutton now made another gift to complement that of the Kress Foundation, which in August 1959 enabled the Friends of Versailles to buy back the embroidered counterpane from Marie-Antoinette's bed in the Queen's State Bedchamber (reopened to the public with its original furnishings and decorations in 1961). Gerald Van der Kemp then married a citizen of the United States, thus strengthening the bonds of friendship that tied him to America and that had made all these exchanges possible.

An American hostess at Versailles

In 1960, at a dinner organized in Paris by the interior decorator Henri Samuel, Gerald Van der Kemp met Florence Harris, who had spent her youth in Washington. A year later, the couple were married in New York. With Florence's three children from her two previous marriages, they moved into the apartments allotted to curators and their families in the Ministers' Wing at Versailles, which they had decorated by Henri Samuel. An accomplished hostess, Mme Van der Kemp now put her talents to the service of Versailles: 'We entertained a great deal; four dinners per month for 60 people, and three lunches for 30. Not to mention the official dinners in the Hall of Mirrors, where guests sat side by side, facing the gardens.' Invitations rapidly became highly sought after, and as a direct result the palace received a number of major donations during the 1960s.

In 1963, David Rockefeller presented a carpet in petit point with a border bearing the arms of France, stitched partly by Marie-Antoinette and her sister-in-law Madame Elisabeth at Versailles, and completed at the Tuileries

A Benefactors' Dinner at Versailles

From 1961, Mme Gerald Van der Kemp succeeded in attracting the attention of great American patrons such as Estée Lauder, seen here with the Begum Aga Khan and Mme Patino.

Large console from the reign of Louis XVI

Some patrons prefer to remain anonymous, such as the benefactor responsible for the gift in 1957 of this large console decorated with military trophies, now in the Apollon Salon.

under the Restoration by Madame Royale and her ladies-in-waiting. In 1965, Florence Gould donated a commode by Macret, and in 1968 Consuelo Vanderbilt, wife of Colonel Jacques Balsan and former Duchess of Marlborough, made a gift of two gilt bronze console tables for the Hunters' Dining Room. In the same year, M. Pierre Schlumberger funded the return of a harp, made in 1775 and attributed to Nadermann, to the Queen's Gilded Cabinet, while Mme Léon Barzin, daughter of Mrs. Merriweather-Post, presented the palace with a pair of cabinets with porcelain plaques by Martin Carlin and a replica bust of Maria Leszczynska for the Dauphin's Bedchamber. In 1969, finally, Mr. and Mrs. Charles Lachmann purchased three porcelain vases for the Clock Salon.

While some generous benefactors had no hesitation in relinquishing important pieces from their collections, others demonstrated their attachment to Versailles through financial donations. These included Robert Magowan, heir to the Safeway supermarket chain; the Coca-Cola company (1965); Mr. and Mrs. Graham Mattison (1966); the Anne Payne Foundation; Mr. and Mrs. Nathan Cummings; Mr. and Mrs. Alfred Bloomingdale; Mr. and Mrs. Byron Smith; Peter Payne; ambassador William Blair and his wife; and, last but not least, George Parker, a great lover of Versailles who built a replica of the Petit Trianon in Texas.

As Daniel Meyer, a former curator and close colleague of Gerald Van der Kemp, explains: 'Unlike French donors who generally donate pieces of furniture, American benefactors prefer to make financial gifts.' The urgency of establishing an American-based foundation — which would allow benefactors to set half of the value of their gifts against tax, in accordance with U.S. financial legislation — thus became all the more pressing.

Commode in painted metal by Macret

In 1965, Florence Gould presented the museum with a metal commode painted in imitation of Chinese lacquer.

**Graham Mattison
at Versailles**

Some friends
of Versailles prefer
to make financial
gifts, such as
Graham Mattison,
seen here with
Baronne de L'Espée.

**Mrs. Albert Lasker
at Versailles**

In 1970, thanks to their
connections in the Nixon
administration, Gerald
and Florence Van der
Kemp created the
Versailles Foundation,
enabling them to appeal
to new benefactors such
as Mrs. Albert Lasker,
seen here with
Gerald Van der Kemp.

The Versailles

Foundation

By virtue of his wife's connections in the Nixon administration, including notably the president's advisor Pat Buchanan and Governor John Connally, in 1970 Gerald Van der Kemp was at last able to set up the 'Versailles Foundation', thus giving form to an idea that had always been close to his heart. In a blue presentation volume, published in 1972, he dwelt eloquently and persuasively on the historic ties that existed between Versailles and America, and on the urgent need for immediate aid: 'Only a handful of craftsmen still know how to use traditional techniques to restore hangings and carpets. Only one or two sculptors and gilders who are capable of reconstructing the finely carved furniture destroyed during the Revolution now remain. But if we do not have the necessary money quickly, we greatly fear that their skills will be lost to us forever.'

Benefactors such as Mrs. Albert Lasker, the Honorable and Mrs. Arthur Watson, Mrs. Ellen Lehman, Mr. and Mrs. Joseph Lauder, Baroness von Wrangel, Mr. and Mrs. Alvin Fuller, Mr. and Mrs. Anastassios Fondaras, Mr. Garrick Stephenson, Mr. and Mrs. William Levitt, Mr. and Mrs. Irvin Levy, Mr. Franklin Murphy, Mr. O'Neil Ryan, Mr. and Mrs. Jules Stein, Mr. William Wood Prince, Mr. and Mrs. Charles Munn, Mr. and Mrs. Richard Lounsberry, Mr. George Frelinghuysen, Mr. and Mrs. Harding Lawrence, Mrs. Alistair Keith, Mrs. Vincent Astor, Mr. and Mrs. Oscar Wyatt, Baron and Baroness Hubert von Pantz, Mr. and Mrs. Gordon Getty and the future ambassador to France the Honorable Pamela Harriman and her husband Averell, enabled the Versailles Foundation to acquire a number of pieces of considerable importance. These included the furniture from the Louis XVI Games Room at Saint-Cloud, made by Georges Jacob and bought at public auction at the Hôtel Drouot on 29 November 1973 for the

Armchair and footstool from the Louis XVI Games Room at Saint-Cloud

In 1973, the Réunion des Musées Nationaux and the Versailles Foundation combined their efforts to purchase at public auction the furniture from the Louis XVI Games Room at Saint-Cloud.

La toilette de la Sultane

In 1978, a gift from the Banque Lazard — through its American Lutece Foundation — enabled the museum to buy a very fine Sèvres porcelain plaque after a painting by Amédée Van Loo, from the collection of Louis XVI.

Dauphin's Great Cabinet, and four late eighteenth-century busts of emperors and a pair of seventeenth-century urns purchased at the Mentmore sale initiated by Lord Rosebery in 1977.

The Van der Kemps did not hesitate to solicit the aid of Henry Ford Jr. — who in 1974 delivered a truck for transporting paintings — and in the previous year organized the 'Versailles War', a peaceful competition between ten fashion designers — five French and five American — with as their only weapons the depth of their plunging décolletés and the froth of their flounces. This fashionable event, for which the guest list included the couturier Oscar de la Renta and his wife, Baronne Guy de Rothschild, Princess Grace of Monaco and Mme Bernard Lanvin, raised a total of two hundred thousand dollars.

On 13 June 1980, Gerald and Florence Van der Kemp invited their friends and benefactors to a last reception at Versailles. On her apricot-colored Dior dress, Florence wore the ribbon of the Légion d'Honneur that she had just been awarded. Alfred Bloomingdale observed drily, 'Louis XIV never had so many friends!' A year later, with the impressive restoration of the King's Bedchamber just completed, Gerald Van der Kemp left Versailles to become director of Claude Monet's house and garden at Giverny, reflecting warmly on his years of American benefaction at Versailles: 'American donors are generous and above all disinterested.'[46]

In 1982, Pierre Lemoine, general curator of Versailles, presided over the inauguration of the private apartments on the ground floor, reopened to the public after a restoration campaign costing seventy million francs. In the words of a leading American magazine: 'The dazzling pomp of yesteryear is restored.'

Antique bust of Nero

Since the departure of Gerald Van der Kemp from Versailles in 1980, the Versailles Foundation has continued to enrich the museum with gifts such as a dressing table belonging to Marie-Antoinette, purchased with the aid of Mrs. Charles Wrightsman, and contributing to the acquisition of this bust of Nero in 1990.

George Parker
at Versailles

George Parker's
passion for Versailles
induced him to build
a house inspired
by the Petit Trianon
in the United States.
Here he is seen
with Barbara de Portago,
who now presides over
the Versailles Foundation
alongside her mother,
Mme Gerald
Van der Kemp.

The Versailles Foundation — in which the Van der Kemp family continued to be represented not only by Florence but also by her daughter Barbara de Portago, who had spent her childhood at the palace — continued its work. Thanks to its help, in 1983 a set of Daguerre appliques was restored to its original place in the Louis XVI Games Room; in 1990, a donation from Mrs. Charles Wrightsman enabled the palace to buy back the dressing table from Marie-Antoinette's bedchamber overlooking the Marble Courtyard; in 1991 the Foundation presented a Sèvres porcelain plaque for the Louis XVI Billiard Room; and in 1994 it donated a pair of *bergères* that had belonged to Mme Du Barry for the Petit Trianon. The Foundation also contributed to larger acquisitions, such as a bust of the Emperor Nero from the collection of Cardinal Mazarin, bequeathed by him to Louis XIV and replaced in the Hall of Mirrors in 1990; two ice dishes from the great Louis XVI service at Versailles, returned in 1998; and, above all, the jewel chest of Marie-Antoinette before she became queen, decorated with Sèvres porcelain plaques and made by Martin Carlin in 1770, and now on view in the Salon of the Queen's Nobles (Salon des Nobles de la reine).

Little by little, the empty salons have thus been refurnished and their walls hung with paintings, 'even though only five per cent of the furniture that embellished the palace under the monarchy has been rediscovered today', as Xavier Salmon, one of the curators, observes.

The long and painstaking task of refurnishing the palace, and the parallel work of restoring the interior decorations, has ensured that the palace of Versailles has become a symbol of French arts and crafts and — not surprisingly — the setting in which the French government chooses to honor its most distinguished guests.

Jefferson in Paris

The exceptional use of the palace rooms as film sets helps to complement the museum's resources. In 1994, the American director James Ivory shot *Jefferson in Paris* on the spot where the action took place, in the Hall of Mirrors at Versailles.

Jewel chest of
Marie-Antoinette

One of the most recent
purchases aided by
the Versailles Foundation
is this jewel chest,
an exceptionally fine
example of eighteenth-
century furniture made
for Marie-Antoinette
under the direction of
Martin Carlin.

Palace of Kings and of the People

Versailles,

presidential

residence

On 31 May 1961, John Fitzgerald Kennedy, thirty-fourth president of the United States, made an official visit to France, accompanied by his wife Jacqueline and Secretary of State Dean Rusk. Set against the background of the Cold War and General de Gaulle's will for independence, the visit was a notable success. De Gaulle had laid down in advance the framework for discussions: 'The first thing to be said is that clearly France and the United States are in the same camp. There can be no question of seeking another alliance. Our job now is to decide what France's contribution to this alliance should be.' Versailles naturally occupied the place of honor in the presidential itinerary, with a performance in the Royal Opera on 3 June followed by a gala dinner in the Hall of Mirrors.

For this sumptuous event, Jacqueline Kennedy — queen of the occasion — wore a white silk dress decorated with strass, designed by Hubert de Givenchy, with a tiara by Alexandre. That evening history came full circle for this First Lady of French ancestry, whose forebear Michel Bouvier, a cabinetmaker from Provence, fought in the ranks of Napoleon's army at Waterloo.[47] Having spent a year at the Sorbonne she spoke French, and she deployed her charm with judicious skill to win over de Gaulle — as he recalled in his memoirs: 'Making a couple of great charm with his radiant and cultivated wife, John Kennedy received the warmest of welcomes. Receptions held in Paris and at Versailles were occasions of the greatest splendor.' At the dinner in the Hall of Mirrors, the one hundred and fifty guests sat at a long table decorated with red roses and sweet peas and lit only by the light of torchères. For this glittering occasion, the transcendent magnificence of Versailles thus succeeded in placing culture above political differences.

President Kennedy at Versailles

On 3 June 1961, General de Gaulle received President Kennedy and succumbed to the charm of his wife in the gilded splendor of this most sumptuous of royal palaces.

President Nixon at Versailles

Following the transformation of the Grand Trianon into an official residence for visiting foreign heads of state, President Nixon — shown here with M. and Mme Gerald Van der Kemp — was received there by General de Gaulle in 1969.

The following year, Jacqueline Kennedy received the French Minister of Culture André Malraux in Washington to prepare the way for the *Mona Lisa*, which was flown to the United States under the personal escort of Gerald Van der Kemp in 1963.

Since 24 July 1959, de Gaulle had had his friend and ally André Malraux at his side, with responsibility for cultural affairs. The two men had known each other since 1936, as recounted by Jean Lacouture, when they found themselves sitting next to each other at a screening of Abel Gance's *Napoléon*. The author of *La Condition Humaine* became first Minister of Information and afterwards Minister of State in the Debré government, with a brief to 'make available the major works of humanity, and above all of France, to the greatest possible number of the French people, to ensure the largest possible audience for the nation's cultural heritage, and to foster the creation of the works of art and the spirit that enrich it.'

De Gaulle loved Versailles, mentioning the palace no fewer than forty times in his *Memoirs of Hope*, and confiding to Malraux: 'Versailles had to be built; let us not quibble over the cost of greatness.' Hitherto, France had received foreign heads of state on official visits at the château of Rambouillet, which de Gaulle always found lacking in comfort and convenience. The quest for another official residence began with the Louvre, followed by Vincennes and Les Invalides, but in all these cases the works necessary to bring the buildings up to the necessary standards of comfort were judged too costly. It was Malraux who finally suggested the restoration of the Grand Trianon, the 'little palace of marbre and porphyry with delightful gardens', in Saint-Simon's description, built by Louis XIV to replace the Trianon de Porcelaine in 1687, in order to serve as a private retreat from the court.

President Carter
at Versailles

In 1978, the French President and Mme Valéry Giscard d'Estaing received the American President and Mrs. Jimmy Carter at Versailles. They are shown here on the balcony of the royal chapel.

President Reagan
at Versailles

Ronald Reagan was the last president of the United States to be received officially at Versailles, on the occasion of the summit of the world's industrialized nations in 1982. Here a guard of honor of the Garde Républicaine salutes him as he passes beneath the colonnade of the Grand Trianon.

In August 1961, General de Gaulle visited the palace and was convinced by Malraux's plans: the left wing of the Grand Trianon would be reserved for the Republic's guests of honor, while the Trianon-sous-Bois wing, in which Louis XIV had installed his sister-in-law 'Madame', his nephew the Duc de Chartres and his three daughters, would be at the disposal of the French president. To release the necessary funds, Malraux presented two programs of legislation to parliament, on 31 July 1962 and 22 November 1963. Estimated originally at twenty million francs, the cost of the works was to more than double, eventually reaching fifty million francs.

Marc Saltet, architect to the Monuments Historiques, supervised the restoration work, while Gerald Van der Kemp oversaw the historic reconstruction of the rooms and Jean Coural, administrator of the Mobilier National, assembled the furniture and First Empire *objets d'art* which would furnish them. At last, on 28 April 1966, the restored building, a majestic affair of pink marble from the Languedoc and green from the Pyrenees, was officially inaugurated by the President of the Republic. Thus, through the initiative of General de Gaulle, the Grand Trianon followed the great palace of Versailles in rediscovering its original role as a palace where the French nation could receive visiting heads of state and foreign dignitaries.

Invited to dine at the Grand Trianon on 1 March 1969, Richard Nixon became the first President of the United States to discover 'this exceedingly rare and valuable ensemble of paneling illustrating the taste of the end of Louis XIV's reign.'[48] In his memoirs, Nixon recalls this superb dinner at Versailles: '... De Gaulle and I met in the Grand Trianon Palace at Versailles. "Louis XIV ruled Europe from this room," he said, as we stood at one of

The Splendors of Versailles exhibition, Jackson, Mississippi

The success enjoyed by this exibition staged in 1998 is an indication of the importance accorded to the palace of the French kings in the heart of the United States.

The 'King's Bedchamber' at Jackson

The quality of the collaboration between the exhibition organizers and the curators at Versailles enabled the museum to send exceptional pieces from its collections to Jackson, including Savonnerie carpets and Gobelins tapestries from the *Histoire du Roi* series.

the huge windows looking out over acres of formal gardens.'[49] But he reserved his eloquence to shower praise on de Gaulle himself, describing him as shrouded in a halo of majesty and putting on a dazzling performance during their meetings. Of all the heads of state that he had met, none could surpass his extraordinary ability to expound on any subject or any world region with such competence, such intelligence, and occasionally an astonishing degree of wisdom and intuition.[50]

The tradition continued after de Gaulle left office in 1969. Nearly a decade later, on 5 January 1978, President Jimmy Carter and his wife dined at the Grand Trianon in their turn, this time as guests of President Valéry Giscard d'Estaing. A reception in the Hall of Mirrors for five thousand guests from the worlds of the performing arts, literature, and politics brought this memorable evening to a close. In 1982, finally, President François Mitterrand decided to hold the eighth summit meeting of the world's industrialized nations not at Rambouillet, as in 1975, but at Versailles. Under tight security, Versailles thus received the world's heads of state, and most notably President Ronald Reagan. On 6 June, a dinner for two hundred guests, of which images were transmitted round the globe, took place in the Hall of Mirrors, to be followed by a fireworks display in the gardens.

President Bill Clinton has never been to Versailles in his official capacity, and nor will the presidents who will succeed him. For henceforth the distinguished guests of the Republic will be received at the Hôtel de Marigny, former residence of Baron Gustave de Rothschild; on 29 March 1999, President Jacques Chirac took the decision to open to the public the apartments at Grand Trianon that had hitherto been reserved for visiting heads of state.

'Marie-Antoinette's Cabinet' at Jackson, Mississippi

Alongside treasures brought to the United States from the palace, *the Splendors of Versailles* exhibition also included pieces from the collections of American museums.

The Hunters' Dining Room at Versailles

The donation made by the Mississippi Commission for International Cultural Exchange following the *Splendors of Versailles* exhibition will fund the restoration of two royal interiors, the Hunters' Dining Room (Salle-à-manger des Retours de Chasse) shown here, and the Dogs Antechamber (Antichambre ou Cabinet des chiens).

The new

American

patronage

In the city of Jackson, Mississippi on 1 August 1998, the Stars and Stripes and the tricolour flag of the French Republic fluttered side by side and a discreet perfume of fleur-de-lis wafted on the breeze. For five months the state capital, formerly part of the great territory of Louisiana, was to host an impressive exhibition organized by Jack Kyle, director of the Mississippi Commission for International Cultural Exchange, and entitled 'Splendors of Versailles'.

For the first time, some 150 prestigious pieces such as Hyacinthe Rigaud's portrait of Louis XIV, the *Création du Monde* clock and the set of Gobelins tapestries entitled *L'Histoire du Roi* had left the palace to be boarded on specially chartered planes. In the immense temporary exhibition hall erected in Jackson, palace craftsmen and local workmen labored side by side to create the most faithful reconstructions possible of the Dogs Antechamber, the King's State Bedchamber, the Hall of Mirrors and Marie-Antoinette's Cabinet, thus allowing visitors who might never visit the true Versailles a glimpse of the sumptuousness of its decorations. The walls were lined with paneling, made in America, with paintwork in imitation of the grey patina of Trianon completing the illusion.

In that summer of 1998, Versailles came to America. In order to persuade the French authorities to authorize these exceptional loans, the Mississippi Commission had undertaken to make a gift to the palace of one million dollars, to be used for the restoration of the Dogs Antechamber, where Louis XV bred his favorite greyhounds, and of the Hunters' Dining Room. Flanking the entrance to the Arts Pavilion in Jackson was a replica of the equestrian statue of Louis XIV of which the original, created by Gianlorenzo Bernini in 1665, is on display in the Orangery at Versailles. While the palace curators

La Paix by
Jean-Baptiste Tuby

The American association the Friends of Vieilles Maisons Françaises not only supports private houses but also contributes to restoration work at Versailles, in 1992 for instance funding the restoration of the sculptures flanking the palace entrance gates.

readily agree to lend works of art to American museums, a loan on such a scale was nevertheless quite exceptional.

The Jackson exhibition is a conspicuous example of the new interest now being shown in Versailles by America. As the twentieth century draws to a close, American patronage — representing an annual average of five million francs — derives from a number of different sources. Traditional benefactors — such as the late Proctor Jones, who died in 1999, whose donations included notably a chandelier for the Hall of Mirrors engraved with his name and that of his wife — are now becoming increasingly rare.

Their place is being taken by associations such as the Friends of French Art under the presidency of Mrs. Elin Vanderlip, and the Friends of Vieilles Maisons Françaises, a philanthropic organization which appeals to the generosity of the American public in order to restore private French châteaux. In 1992, for example, this association funded the restoration of two allegorical sculptures flanking the gates to the Cour d'Honneur, *La Victoire sur l'Empire* (1680-1) by Gaspard and Balthazar Marsy, and *La Paix* (1681-3) by Jean-Baptiste Tuby. Another such organization, the World Monuments Fund France, is shortly to finance the restoration of Marie-Antoinette's theater at Trianon.

'Nowadays pure patronage no longer exists, or only very rarely. Donors now receive something in exchange for their gifts: private visits to the palace, the hire of certain rooms for private receptions, the loan of certain works. People talk more readily of sponsorship than of patronage,' explains Hubert Astier, President of the Etablissement Public du Domaine et du Musée National du château de Versailles et des Trianons, who, with a budget of 240 million francs, is responsible for the upkeep of 200,000 square metres

The Man in the Iron Mask

Louis XIV and the history of France continue to inspire Hollywood. In 1998, Leonardo DiCaprio played the double role of the Sun King and the mysterious prisoner in the film directed by Randall Wallace.

La Victoire sur l'Empire

The restoration of this
sculpture by Gaspard
and Balthazar Marsy
was also funded
by the Friends of Vieilles
Maisons Françaises.

of buildings, 100,000 square metres of roof and 850 hectares of gardens. This outside support, even when tied to services in return, now forms an indispensable complement to the annual budget, which is devoted essentially to the maintenance of the buildings and gardens. Thanks to this private aid, the curators are able to continue to implement a policy put in place in 1980, striving whenever possible to bring back to the palace its original furnishings, generally identified at large auction sales. Thus at the sale of furniture and *objets d'art* from the collection of Gouverneur Morris, the museum of Versailles acquired for the Queen's Billiard Room a pair of sofas that had once belonged to Marie-Antoinette.

But we now live in an era when protection of the environment and a renewed interest in nature have become priorities, and in a sign of the times American patrons, formerly so generous in their support of the palace buildings, are now displaying even more interest in the gardens. Louis XIV would surely have approved of this new concern, for in his own view the gardens were one of the principal *raisons d'être* of Versailles. Constructed around the myth of Apollo, Greek god of light and the sun, these allegorical pleasure grounds form a self-contained universe to which the Sun King himself provided the ultimate guide in his *Manière de montrer les jardins de Versailles*, written in 1689.

The restoration of the King's Potager, created by Jean-Baptiste de La Quintinye in 1678-83 to supply the palace kitchens with fruit and vegetables, is a first step in this direction. In 1993, a gift from the World Monuments Fund France, under its then-president Hubert de Givenchy, financed the repair and regilding of the Grille du Roy, the oldest gates at Versailles,

Marie-Antoinette's theater

Following the restoration of the King's Potager led by M. Hubert de Givenchy, with the help of Mrs. Paul Mellon, the World Monuments Fund, many of whose members are American, is considering adding its support to the forthcoming restoration of Marie-Antoinette's theater at Trianon.

made in 1681 by Alexis Fordrin, while another from Mrs. Paul Mellon enabled work to start on the above-mentioned restoration of the palace kitchen gardens which still remain in use.

In 1998 on the initiative of Catherine Hamilton, a passionate Chicago-based francophile and member of the Société des Amis de Versailles, a new organization was founded under the name of the American Friends of Versailles. As its first project, it chose to fund the replanting and reconstruction of the Bosquet des Trois Fontaines, designed by Le Nôtre in 1679 and destroyed without trace two centuries ago. 'These bosquets were in fact outdoor *salons* in which the king gave entertainments and concerts. They took the form of small square groves of trees with clearings at their centre embellished with architectural features, topiary and fountains,' explains Pierre-André Lablaude, architect-in-chief to the Monuments Historiques and responsible for the gardens at Versailles today. He goes on to caution: 'Gardens *à la française* are frequently represented as strict and austere; in fact, by virtue of these ephemeral embellishments of plants and trees and of fountains which have now disappeared, they were exuberantly baroque in feel.' The American Friends of Versailles, which on 26 June 1999 gave a grand ball at Versailles as a gesture of thanks to its patrons, plans to raise four million dollars to finance this restoration project, which is due to be completed in 2001.

In a country where cultural institutions receive no state funding, Americans make a noble habit of contributing to such ventures. Charities are able to mobilize a tremendous amount of energy, and in the year 1998 alone raised donations of 120 billion dollars. Encouraged by a financial system that

The Bosquet
des Trois Fontaines

Under the aegis of
Mrs. David Hamilton,
a new association,
the American Friends
of Versailles, is
helping to finance
the restoration
of the Bosquet des
Trois Fontaines,
beneath the palace walls.

favors such donations, Americans give generously. But the exceptional level of American patronage from which Versailles has benefited may ultimately be explained only by the evocative image of this unique palace and park — a crossroads of the common history of two great nations — on the far side of the Atlantic. Three centuries after he created these remarkable gardens, at once classical and baroque in inspiration, André Le Nôtre would no doubt be moved by this unprecedented mobilization of transatlantic energy and funds aimed at restoring them to life.

Conclusion

Included by Unesco on its list of monuments forming part of the heritage of humanity, Versailles is a site of considerable prestige which receives an annual total of five million visitors to the gardens and three and a half million to the palace. Among foreign visitors, Americans make up the greatest number. As in the time of Louis XIV, the gardens are crowded with life once more: 'We are not like private citizens; we owe ourselves entirely to our public,' the Sun King was given to remark, retiring to Marly when he desired privacy. Nowadays, as visitors from every American state stroll through the Vestibule Gabriel and the adjoining gallery on their way to the Musée Louis-Philippe, they may pause to read inscribed in the stone the names of their compatriots who have helped to restore life to Versailles. Soon in the gardens, thanks to the generosity of new benefactors, they will be able to enjoy the fountains playing in the Bosquet of the Three Fountains, just as they did in the time of Louis XIV.

The continuity of history is thus also that of the relationship — sometimes turbulent but always peaceful — that binds France and America.

Ball at Versailles, 26 June 1999

Seen at a reception given by the American Friends of Versailles are M. Hubert Astier — President of the Etablissement Public du Domaine et du Musée National de Versailles —, Mme Jacques Chirac, Mrs. David Hamilton, the Vicomte de Rohan — President of the Société des Amis de Versailles — and M. Pierre Arizzoli-Clémentel — General Director of the Etablissement Public du Domaine et du Musée National de Versailles.

The American Friends of Versailles in the Bosquet des Trois Fontaines

The restoration of the Bosquet des Trois Fontaines is being preceded by archaeological excavations revealing the remains of this once famous water feature.

American Benefactors

Among the American benefactors, past and present, who have been generous in their support of Versailles are:

The American Friends of Versailles
The Honorable and Mrs. Walter Annenberg
Mr. George Ansley
Mr. and Mrs. Robert Arnold
Mrs. Vincent Astor
Mr. and Mrs. H. Bagley
Mrs. C. Balderich
Madame Jacques Balsan,
   formerly Duchess of Marlborough
Judge P. T. Barlow
Mme Léon Barzin
Anne H. Bass
Mrs. Kenneth Bilby
Major Armand D. Blackley
The Honorable and
   Mrs. William McCormick Blair
Mrs. S. D. Bliss
Mr. and Mrs. Alfred Bloomingdale
Shotaro Charles de Bourbon
Mr. Robert D. Brewster
Mr. and Mrs. S. Brody
The Yvonne P. and Robert M. Brown III
   Foundation
The Honorable and Mrs. David K.E. Bruce
Mr. and Mrs. John H. Bryan - Sara Lee
Mr. Claus von Bulow
Mr. P. Burns.
Mr. Edward Lee Cave
Mr. and Mrs. Gardiner Cowles
The Honorable Anne Cox Chambers
Mrs. Robert Charles
The Coca Cola Company
Governor and Mrs. John Connally

Ms Franci Crane
Mr. and Mrs. James Crown
Mr. and Mrs. Nathan Cummings
Mr. and Mrs. Walter De Lear
The Honorable and Mrs. Douglas Dillon
Mr. and Mrs. James Donnelley
Mr. and Mrs. Clyde Engle
Mrs. C. Englehard
Mr. and Mrs. Anastassios Fondaras
Mr. and Mrs. Christopher Forbes
Mr. and Mrs. Henry Ford II
Mrs. Alice Fordyce
Mr. Forsyth Wickes
Mr. Carl Forsythe
Mr. George Frelinghuysen
French & Company
Mr. and Mrs. Richard Friedberg
The Friends of Vieilles Maisons Françaises
Mr. and Mrs. Alvin Fuller
Mr. and Mrs. James Fullerton
Mrs. George F. Getty II
Mr. and Mrs. Gordon Getty
Mr. and Mrs. Burt A. Getz
Mr. and Mrs. Ronald Gidwitz
Mr. and Mrs. Richard A. Giesen
Ms. Curry Glassell-Roberts
Mrs. Florence Gould
The Florence Gould Foundation
Mrs. Dolly Green
Mr. Alexis Gregory
Mrs. John Gutfreund
Mr. and Mrs. M. Hall
Mr. and Mrs. David R. Hamilton
Mr. and Mrs. Samuel C. Hamilton
The Honorable Averell and
   the Honorable Pamela Harriman

Mr. and Mrs. King Harris
Mrs. Walter A. Haas
Mr. and Mrs. Thomas Hassen
Mrs. Ira Haupt
Mr. and Mrs. Henry Heinz II
Mrs. Eugenia W. Hitt
Mr. and Mrs. William Hood -
   American Airlines
Mrs. S. Hooker
Mrs. Barbara Hutton
The Honorable and Mrs. Proctor P. Jones
Mr. and Mrs. John W. Jordan II
The Herman and Ruth Kahn Foundation
Mr. Ernest Kanzler
Mr. Lehman Katz
Mr. William Keighley
Mrs. Alistair Keith
Ms. Karen Keland
The Kellen Foundation
The Kemper Foundation
Mr. and Mrs. R. Kidder
Mr. and Mrs R. Kiesling
Mr. and Mrs F.B. Kingsbury
Dr. and Mrs. Henry Kissinger
Mr. R.F. Knoedler
Mr. and Mrs. Frederick Krehbiel - Molex
The Kress Foundation
Mr. Rushmore Kress
Mr. and Mrs. Charles Lachmann
Mrs. Albert Lasker
Mr. and Mrs. Joseph Lauder
Mr. and Mrs. Harding Lawrence
Mr. and Mrs. John Ridings Lee
Mrs. Ellen Lehman
Lehman Brothers
M and Mrs. William Levitt

Appendices

1. Olive Dickason *Le mythe du sauvage* Editions Septentrion, Quebec 1993, p.21.
2. ibid. p.230.
3. ibid. p.231.
4. *L'Amérique continent imprévu*, under the supervision of Daniel Lévine, Bordas, Paris 1992.
5. Huguette Joris-Zavala in the catalogue of the exhibition *Mémoire de l'Amérique*, Musée du Nouveau Monde, La Rochelle 1980.
6. Anne Vitart *Curiosités américaines* in *L'Amérique continent imprévu*, op.cit.
7. '*L'Amérique baroque*' in the catalogue of the exhibition *L'Amérique vue par l'Europe* at the Grand Palais, Paris 17 September 1976 to 3 January 1977.
8. Révérend Père Louis Hennepin *Description de la Louisiane*, Paris 1688.
9. Père François-Xavier de Charlevoix *Memoirs* VI:177-8.
10. Duc de Saint-Simon *La Cour de Louis XIV*, pp.485-7.
11. André Kaspi Les Américains I, p.99 Paris.
12. John Adam on Franklin 15 May 1811, in J.A.Leo Lemay and P.M Zau *Benjamin Franklin, Autobiography*, Norton, New York 1986.
13. M. le Comte de Ségur *Mémoires ou souvenirs et anecdotes* I pp.116-17.
14. Bernard Vincent *Histoire des Etats-Unis*, Nancy 1994, p.53.
15. Jeanne-Louise Henriette Campan (Genêt) *Mémoires sur la vie de Marie-Antoinette*, Paris, Firmin Didot, no date, quoted in Bruno Cortequisse *La Galerie des glaces*, Paris 1999.
16. Alfred Owen Alridge *Franklin and his French Contemporaries*, New York University Press 1957, p.43.
17. Quoted in Esmond Wright *Franklin of Philadelphia* Harvard 1986, p.260.
18. Ronald W. Clark *Benjamin Franklin*, Paris 1986.
19. William Howard Adams *The Paris Years of Thomas Jefferson*, Yale University Press 1997.
20. *Les officiers de l'Armée américaine par le présent acte et de façon la plus solennelle s'associent et se constituent en sociétés d'amis*. On 13 May 1783, the Prussian Baron Steuben created the Order of Cincinnati, named after the Roman Lucius Quintus Cincinnatus, at an official ceremony at the headquarters of the American armies on the banks of the Hudson River. Article 27 recognized French members such as the Chevalier de La Luzerne, the Comte d'Estaing, the Comte de Grasse and the Comte de Rochambeau.
21. Letter from the architect Heurtier, addressed to Angiviller and quoted in Christian Baulez *Notes on a few pieces of furniture and objects that belonged in Louis XVI and Marie-Antoinette's private apartments*.
22. Philip Boucher *Les Nouvelles Frances - France in America 1500-1815, an Imperial Perspective*, Rhode Island 1989.
23. Quoted in *Curiosités américaines*, op. cit.
24. Jean Orieux *Talleyrand*, Flammarion, Paris 1970.
25. Louis-Philippe *Journal de mon voyage en Amérique*, Flammarion, Paris 1976.
26. ibid.
27. Letter from John Vanderlyn to his brother Peter dated 14 August 1797, quoted in Kevin Avery and Peter Fodera *John Vanderlyn's Panoramic View of the Palace and Gardens of Versailles*, Metropolitan Museum of Art, New York 1988.
28. William Howard Adams *The Paris Years of Thomas Jefferson*, op. cit.
29. Mark Laird *Formal Gardens: Traditions of Art and Nature*, London.
30. ibid.
31. George Catlin *Notes on eight years of travel and residence in Europe* quoted in *Sur le sentier de la découverte. Rencontres franco-indiennes du XVIᵉ au XXᵉ siècle*, exhibition catalogue 27 June to 12 October 1992. Musée National de la Coopération Franco-Américaine, Château de Blérancourt.
32. Reception for the Iowa Indians at the Tuileries, as related by George Catlin, *Catalogue de la galerie Indienne*, Paris 1845.
33. Thomas W. Gaetgens *Versailles, de la Résidence Royale au musée historique*, Albin Michel, Paris.
34. Quoted in Charles Zorgbibe *Wilson, un croisé à la Maison Blanche*, Presses des Sciences Politiques, Paris 1998
35. Warwick Greene *Letters of Warwick Greene 1875-1928*, Houghton Mifflin Company, The Riverside Press, Cambridge 1931, p.106.
36. Bruno Cortequisse *La Galerie des Glaces de Louis XIV à nos jours*, Perrin, Paris 1999, p.242.
37. Quoted in *Letters of Warwick Greene*, op. cit., p.109.
38. Janet Flaner *Paris was Yesterday*, Penguin.
39. Jane S. Smith *Elsie de Wolfe*, Athaeneum, New York 1982.
40. James T. Maher *The Twilight of Splendor*, Little Brown, New York 1975.
41. ibid. p.376.
42. Françoise Ouzan *Un exemple d'engagement : l'American Hospital de Reims 1919-1947* in *Les Américains et la France 1917-1947*, Maisonneuve et Larousse 1999.
43. Letter published in *Le Figaro* 30 May 1924 and in the *American Magazine of Art*, November 1925.
44. R. Coureau *Rockefeller roi des pétroles*, Payot, Paris 1934.
45. Interview with Gerald Van der Kemp by journalist Jean des Cars in *Le Figaro Magazine*.
46. Interview with Charles Bricker in *Harpers and Queen*, January 1981.
47. Obliged to flee France at the Restoration, Michel Bouvier emigrated to America, where he settled in Philadelphia. There his first client was Joseph Bonaparte, brother of Napoleon and another French émigré, who now resided at the Delaware estate of Fort Breeze, which he had filled with Empire furniture.
48. Pierre Arrizoli-Clémentel, Directeur Général de l'Etablissement Public du Domaine et du Musée National de Versailles, press conference, 29 March 1999.
49. Richard Nixon *The Memoirs of Richard Nixon*, Grosse and Dunlap, New York 1978.
50. Richard Nixon *Leaders*, quoted in Jean Lacouture *De Gaulle : Part 3 Le Souverain*, Le Seuil, Paris 1986.

Select Bibliography

Part I

VERSAILLES AND AMERICA BEFORE THE TWENTIETH CENTURY

Chapter I. France sets out to conquer America

L'Amérique vue par l'Europe, exhibition catalogue, Paris 1976

ARCINIEGAS, German, *America in Europe: a History of the New World in Reverse*, San Diego 1986

ATKINSON, Geoffrey, *The Extraordinary Voyage in French Literature*, vol.I, before 1700, New York 1920

BOUCHER, Philip, *Les Nouvelles Frances-France in America 1500-1815: An Imperial Perspective*, Rhode Island 1989

BUZHARDT, Gail Alexandra and HAWTHORNE, Margaret, *Encounters on the Mississippi 1682-1763*, Jackson 1993

CAMPAN, Jeanne Louise Henriette, *Mémoires sur la vie de Marie-Antoinette*, Firmin Didot, Paris (n.d)

CHESNEL, Pierre, *Histoire de Cavelier de La Salle*, Paris 1900

DICKASON, Olive, *Le mythe du sauvage*, Quebec 1993

ELLIOT, J.H., *First Images of America: the impact of the New World on the Old*, Berkeley 1976

ERLANGER, Philippe, *Louis XIV*, Paris 1965

LAVISSE, Ernest, *Louis XIV*, Paris 1989

LEVINE, Daniel (ed) *L'Amérique continent imprévu*, Paris 1992

ORDHAL KUPPERMANN, Karen, *America in European Consciousness*, North Carolina 1995

VITART FARDOULIS, Anne, *Les objets indiens des collections royales: le Canada de Louis XIV*, Saint-Germain-en-Laye 1980

Chapter II. France champions the United States

ALREDGE, Alfred Owen, *Franklin and his French Contemporaries*, New York 1957

BOWERS, Claude, *Young Jefferson*, Boston 1945

CASTRIES, Duc de, *'Qu'est ce qu'un Cincinnati?'*, *Historia*, no.151, June 1959

CLARK, Ronald W., *Benjamin Franklin*, Empartners A.G. 1983

CORTEQUISSE, Bruno, *La Galerie des Glaces*, Paris 1999

GOUTEL, Baron HENNET de, *'Les Etats-Unis à Versailles'*, *Je sais tout*, 11 August 1917

KASPI, André, *Les Américains*, Paris 1986

LEMAY, J.A. Leo and ZAU, P.M, *Benjamin Franklin's Autobiography*, New York 1986

VINCENT, Bernard, *Histoire des Etats-Unis*, Nancy 1994

Chapter III. Versailles and America: from Louis XVI to Louis-Philippe

ADAMS, William Howard, *The Paris Years of Thomas Jefferson*, Yale 1997

AVERY, Kevin and FODERA, Peter, *John Vanderlyn's Panoramic View of the Palace and Gardens of Versailles*, New York 1988

CHINARD, Gilbert, *L'Amérique et le rêve exotique dans la littérature française*, Paris 1913

FOHLEN, Claude, *Jefferson à Paris*, Paris 1957

GÆTGENS, Thomas, *Versailles: de la résidence royale au musée historique*, Antwerp 1984

GIRAUD, Marcel, *Histoire de la Louisiane*, Paris 1957

LAIRD, Mark, *The Formal Garden: Traditions of Art and Nature*, London 1993

LOUIS-PHILIPPE, *Journal de mon voyage d'Amérique*, edited by S. d'Huart and J.P. Babelon, Paris 1976

ORIEUX, Jean, *Talleyrand*, Paris 1970

ROHAN-CHABOT, Alix de, *Madame de La Tour du Pin*, Paris 1997

Part II

VERSAILLES AND AMERICA IN THE TWENTIETH CENTURY

Chapter I. The United States and Versailles

Les Américains et la France 1917-1947, Reims 1999

COUREAU, R., *Rockefeller roi des pétroles*, Paris 1934

DAWSON, Washington, *'Versailles et les Rockefeller'*, *Revue des deux mondes*, 15 February 1954

GREENE, Warwick, *Letters from Warwick Greene 1915-1928*, Cambridge 1931

MAHER, James T., *The Twilight of Splendor*, New York 1975

MARTIN DU GARD, Maurice, *'Reflets dans la Galerie des glaces'*, *Revue des deux mondes*, July 1955

SALINGER, Pierre, *La France et le nouveau monde*, Paris 1976

SMITH, Jane, *Elsie de Wolfe*, New York 1982

ZORGBIBE, Charles, *Wilson, un croisé à la Maison Blanche*, Presses des Sciences Politiques, Paris 1998

Chapter II. The United States supports the Museum of Versailles

Research for this chapter was based largely on newspaper and magazine articles, including the following:

DES CARS, Jean, interviews with Gerald Van der Kemp in *Perspectives* and *Le Figaro Magazine*, 1972.

LAWFORD, Valentine, *'A Fresh Wind through Versailles'*, *Vogue*, August 1967

REIF, Rita, *'The No. 1 dealer of Versailles'*, *New York Times*, 7 January 1979

VAN DER KEMP, Gerald, *Versailles*, Paris 1977

WECHSBERG, Joseph, *'Paris Journal'*, *Gourmet Magazine*, October 1976

Special thanks are due to Mme Gerald Van der Kemp for her helpf and generosity in allowing the author free access to her photograph albums and press cuttings

Chapter III. Palace of Kings and of the People

DAVIS, John, *Jacqueline Bouvier, an intimate Memoir*, New York 1996

LACOUTURE, Jean, *De Gaulle*, Paris 1986

LACOUTURE, Jean, *Malraux*, Paris 1973

Mississippi Commission for International Cultural Exchanges Inc., *Splendors of Versailles*, 1998

NIXON, Richard, *Memoirs of Richard Nixon*, New York 1978

Guides to Versailles

Two particularly helpful guidebooks are:

BABELON, Jean-Pierre; BAJOU, Thierry; CONSTANS, Claire; POUGETOUX, Alain, and SALMON, Xavier, *The Palace of Versailles from A to Z*, Paris 1996

LEMOINE, Pierre, *Guide du musée et domaine national de Versailles et Trianon*, Paris 1991

List of illustrations

The National Gallery of Art, Washington D.C.,
Andrew W. Mellon Collection
Photograph: The National Gallery of Art
Philip A. Charles

page 25
America ('L'Amérique')
Gilles Guérin (1606/9-1678)
Marble, 1675-8
Château de Versailles
Photograph: R.M.N., Daniel Arnaudet

page 27
Char de Triomphe tapestry
After a cartoon by Yvart le père and Baudrain (cartoon painter)
and from a design by Charles Le Brun (1619-90)
Manufacture des Gobelins, 1717
Silk and wool
347cm (H) x 267cm (W)
The J. Paul Getty Museum, Los Angeles
Photograph: The J. Paul Getty Museum, Jack Ross

page 29
The Duchess of Parma and Her Daughter Isabelle
Jean-Marc Nattier (1685-1766)
Oil on canvas, 1750
133cm (H) x 106cm (W)
Hillwood Museum, Washington, D.C.
Photograph: Courtesy of Hillwood Museum and Gardens

Spring
François Boucher (1703-70)
Oil on canvas, 1755.
52.2cm x 73cm
The Frick Collection, New York
Photograph: The Frick Collection

page 31
Architecture and Chemistry
Painting and Sculpture
François Boucher (1703-70)
Oil on canvas, 1750-2
217.2cm x 77.5cm
The Frick Collection, New York
Photograph: The Frick Collection

page 32
Californian lizard
Alexandre-Jean Noël (1752-1834)
Drawing, 1769
Musée du Louvre, Cabinet des dessins
Photograph: R.M.N., J.G. Berizzi

page 33
America ('L'Amérique: Le Kataco, le courlis, la poule sultane et le coq de roche')
Jean-Jacques Bachelier (1724-1806)
Oil on canvas
Muséum National d'Histoire Naturelle, Paris.
Photograph: R.M.N., Daniel Arnaudet.

page 34
Commode by Gilles Joubert (1689-1775)
Oak veneered with kingwood, tulipwood, holly or boxwood, and ebony; gilt-bronze mounts; Sarrancolin marble top, 1769
93cm (H) x 181cm (W) x 673 cm (D)
Made for Madame Louise de France, youngest daughter of Louis XV, for her apartments at the palace of Versailles
The J. Paul Getty Museum, Los Angeles
Photograph: The J. Paul Getty Museum

page 35
Northern America ('L'Amérique septentrionale')
Sketch for the painting by Bachelier for the gallery in the Ministry of Foreign Affairs at Versailles
Jean-Jacques Bachelier (1724-1806)
Gouache on paper, 1762
Bibliothèque Municipale de Versailles
Photograph: Martine Beck-Coppola

page 36
Illustrations on vellum for *'Les arbres de l'Amérique septentrionale'*
by François and Antoine Michaux
Bignonia catalpa by P.Bessa, plate 116
Rhododendron maximum by P. Bessa, plate 103
Pinus strobus by P. Bessa, plate 10
Bibliothèque Centrale du Muséum National d'Histoire Naturelle, Ms 328
Photograph: Cop. Bibliothèque centrale M.N.H.N., Paris

View of the Queen's Hamlet at Trianon,
Claude-Louis Châtelet (1753-94)
Watercolour, 1781
Biblioteca Estense, Modena
Photograph: Gianni Roncaglia

page 37
Illustration on vellum for *'Les arbres de l'Amérique septentrionale'*
by François and Antoine Michaux
Liriodendron tulipifera by P. Bessa, plate 115
Bibliothèque Centrale du Muséum National d'Histoire Naturelle, Ms 328
Photograph: Cop. Bibliothèque centrale M.N.H.N., Paris

page 39
America ('L'Amérique')
Antoine Vestier (1740-1824)
Drawing, second half of the eighteenth century
Château de Blérancourt, Musée National de la Coopération Franco-Américaine
Photograph: R.M.N., Gérard Blot

Chapter II. Versailles champions the United States

page 41
Charles Gravier, Comte de Vergennes, Minister of Foreign Affairs in 1794 (1717-87)
Antoine-François Callet (1741-1823)
Oil on canvas, c.1781
79cm (H) x 61cm (W) - oval
Château de Versailles
Photograph: R.M.N., Daniel Arnaudet-J. Schormans

Marie Gilbert du Motier, Marquis de La Fayette, in his uniform as captain of the Noailles Regiment
Léopold-Louis Boilly (1761-1845)
Oil on canvas, 1788
Château de Versailles
Photograph: R.M.N., Daniel Arnaudet - J. Schormans

page 43
La Fayette embarks for America
Hubert Robert (1733-1808)
Oil on canvas, c.1800
Château de Blérancourt, Musée National de la Coopération Franco-Américaine
Photograph: R.M.N., Gérard Blot

Page 45
Commode by David Roentgen (1743-1807) - front view and details of the side panels
Veneered on oak and pine with tulipwood, sycamore, box-wood, purplewood, pearwood, harewood, and other woods; gilt-bronze mounts; red brocatelle marble top
89.5cm (H) x 135.9cm (W) x 69.2cm (D)
The Metropolitan Museum of Art, New York. The Jack and Belle Linsky Collection, 1982
Photograph: The Metropolitan Museum of Art

page 46
Benjamin Franklin
Sketch attributed to Joseph Siffred Duplessis
Oil on canvas, 1778
Musée Carnavalet, Paris
Photograph: Photothèque des Musées de la Ville de Paris, P. Pierrain

The Reception of Benjamin Franklin at Versailles
W.O. Geller
Engraving, printed by Baron Jolly in 1830
Beinecke Library, Yale University
Photograph: Beinecke Library, Yale University

page 47
Hôtel de Valentinois,
Attibuted to Antoine Pérignon
Gouache
Château de Blérancourt, Musée National de la Coopération Franco-Américaine
Photograph: R.M.N.

page 48
Set of three Sèvres vases
Sèvres Manufactory, c.1780
Painted by Antoine Caton († 1798),
enamel jewelling by Philippe Parpette,
gilded by Etienne-Henry Le Guay père (1719/20-99)
Height: 49.6 cm (vase I), 40.8cm (vase II), 40.5cm (vase III)
'Vases des âges : vase des âges à têtes de vieillards, première grandeur; vases des âges à têtes de jeunes femmes, deuxième grandeur'
The J. Paul Getty Museum, Los Angeles
Photograph: The J. Paul Getty Museum

page 49
Pair of vases, painted by Caton
Sèvres Manufactory, 1779
Hard-paste porcelain decorated in polychrome enamels and gold
Height: 71 cm
Museum of Fine Arts, Boston
Bequest of Miss Elizabeth Howard Bartol (right)
Gift of the Heirs of Helen Jaques (left)
Photograph: courtesy Museum of Fine Arts, Boston

page 51
The 'Independence' coiffure ('La coiffure de l'Indépendance' ou 'Le Triomphe de la Liberté')
Unknown artist
Colored engraving, c.1780
Château de Blérancourt, Musée National de la Coopération Franco-Américaine
Photograph: R.M.N., Gérard Blot

page 52
George Washington
Gilbert Stuart (1755-1828)
Oil on canvas, 1795-6.
74.3cm (H) x 60.9cm (W)
The Frick Collection, New York.
Photograph: The Frick Collection

page 53
John Paul Jones
Jean-Antoine Houdon (1741-1828)
Plaster, 1780
Château de Blérancourt, Musée National de la Coopération Franco-Américaine
Photograph: R.M.N., Gérard Blot

Philippe-Henri-Marie, Marquis de Ségur, Maréchal de France (1724-1801)
Louise-Elisabeth Vigée-Lebrun (1755-1842)
Oil on canvas, c.1789
115cm (H) x 81cm (W)
Château de Versailles
Photograph: R.M.N.

Jean-Baptiste-Donatien de Vimeur, Comte de Rochambeau (1725-1807)
Charles-Philippe Larivière (1798-1876)

Oil on canvas, 1834
214cm (H) x 140cm (W)
Château de Versailles
Photograph: R.M.N., D. Daniel Arnaudet / G. B.

page 54
Robinson House, Newport, Rhode Island
Photograph - Private collection
Photograph: Jean Chenel

page 55
The Vicomte de Noailles (1756-1804)
Gilbert Stuart (1755-1828)
Oil on canvas, 1798
127cm (H) x 101.6cm (W)
The Metropolitan Museum of Art, New York. Purchase, Henry R. Luce Gift, Elihu Root Jr. Bequest, Rogers Fund, Maria DeWitt Jesup Fund, Morris K. Jesup Fund, and Charles and Anita Blatt Gift, 1970
Photograph: The Metropolitan Museum of Art

The Siege of Yorktown, 6-19 October 1781
Louis-Nicolas Van Blarenberghe (1716-94)
Gouache on paper, 59cm (H) x 94cm (W)
Château de Versailles
Photograph: R.M.N., P. Bernard

page 57
The Departure ('Le Départ')
Pierre-Alexandre Wille le fils (1748-1821)
Oil on canvas, 1785
Château de Blérancourt, Musée National de la Coopération Franco-Américaine
Photograph: R.M.N., Gérard Blot

page 59
Arbor at West Point
Boston Public Library
Photograph: Boston Public Library

Proclamation of the Treaty of Paris in front of the Tuileries, 25 November 1783
Anton Van Ysendyck (1801-75)
Oil on canvas, c.1837
79cm (H) x 144 cm (W)
Château de Versailles
Photograph: R.M.N., Gérard Blot

175

Index

177

Acknowledgements

The publisher and the author wish to express their gratitude to M. Philippe Pascal and Mrs. Mireille Guiliano, whose generous assistance has made the publication of this work possible.

For their invaluable help and support they would like to extend their thanks to the following:
LL. AA. RR. Monseigneur
le Comte de Paris † and
Madame la Comtesse de Paris
M. Victor Barcimanto
M. Stéphane Castelluccio
Mme Séverine Gallet-Burgelin
Mrs. David Hamilton
M. Gérard Mabille
Monsieur le Duc and
Madame la Duchesse de Mouchy
Mr. Edgar Munhall
Baronne Elie de Rothschild
Mme Gerald Van der Kemp
Mme Pascal Zuber

Château de Versailles
M. Pierre Arizzoli-Clémentel
M. Hubert Astier
M. Christian Baulez
Mlle Claire Constans
M. Frédéric Didier
Mlle Annick Heitzmann
Mme Simone Hoog
M. Pierre-André Lablaude
Mme Ariane de Lestrange
M. Xavier Salmon

Bibliothèque Municipale de Versailles
Mlle Rose

Bibliothèque du Muséum National d'Histoire Naturelle
Mme Ducreux
Mme Heurtel

Musée National de la Coopération Franco-Américaine, château de Blérancourt
Mme Dopffer

Musée de la Toile de Jouy
Mlle Anne de Thoisy

The Hillwood Museum, Washington D.C.
Mrs. Anne Odom

The J. Paul Getty Museum, Los Angeles
Mrs. Charissa Bremer David
Mrs. Jacklyn Burns
Mrs. Gillian Wilson

The Metropolitan Museum of Art, New York
Mr. Tom Campbell
Mrs. Deanna D. Cross
Mr. James Draper
Mr. Jared Goss
Mrs. Heather Lemonedes
Mrs. Doralynn Pines
Mr. William Rieder
Mrs. Eileen Sullivan
Mr. Gary Tinterow
Mrs. Julie Zeftel

The Mississippi Commission for International Cultural Exchange
Mr. Jack Kyle

The Museum of Fine Arts, Boston
Mrs. Elizabeth Fiorentino
Mrs. Karen L. Otis
Mrs. Anne Poulet
Mrs. Mary L. Sluskonis

The National Gallery, Washington D.C.
Mrs. Alyson Luchs
Mrs. Sara Sanders-Buell
Mrs. Nancy Stanfield

The New York Historical Society
Ms. Gotbaun
Mr. Paul Gunther
Mrs. Margaret Heilbrun
Mrs. Nicole Wells

The Preservation Society of Newport County
Mr. Paul Miller
Mr. John Tschirch

M. Sylvain Alliod
Mr. William Ambler
Mme Violette Andrès
Mme Beck-Coppola
M. Sylvain Bellenger
M. Louis Benech
Mme Bertrand
M. Antoine Cahen
Mrs. Theresa Canora
M. Ralph Carpenter
M. Hervé Cassan
Mme Roselyne de Castéja
M. Bruno Centorame
Mlle Catherine Challot
Comte de Chambrun
M. Jean Chenel
M. Bernd Dams
M. Serge Darmon
Mrs. Eleanor DeLorme
M. Gérard Delorme
Mme Jean Ducamp
Mr. Martin Durrant
Mrs. Melody Ennis
M. Alain Escourbiac
M. and Mme Michel Escourbiac
M. Philippe Escourbiac
M. Olivier Eyquem
Mme Faroux
Mr. Dan Farrell
Mme Anne de Fayet
Mme Galéa
Mme Anne-Marie de Ganay
Mme Robert Gillet

Miss Holland Goss
Mme Henri Grandcolas
Mme Stéphane Guégan
Mrs. John Gutfreund
Sir Gavin Harding
Mme Houssenbey
Comte Ghislain d'Humières
Mr. Mark D. Hunter
M. Pierre Jacky
M. Pierrick Jan
Mr. Kevin L. Krueger
Princesse Georges-Henri de
La Tour d'Auvergne Lauraguais
Mme Jacqueline Lefrançois
Baron François Le Vert
Mme Lindsay
M. Dominique Lobstein
M. Henri Loyrette
Mr. Adam Marchand
M. Claude Mastantuono
M. and Mme Jean-François Méjanès
Mme Jean-Bernard Mérimée
M. Daniel Meyer
Mr. Davitt Moroney
Ms. Oliver
M. Michel Passet
Mlle Pauly
Mme Béatrice Petit
Mrs. Barbara de Portago
M. Alexandre Pradère
Mme Maxime Préaud
Mme Charlotte Riou
Mme Caroline Roboh
M. Jean-Pierre Samoyault
Mrs. Lynne Sheldon
Mr. Jason Stein
M. Gabriel Terrades-Pujol
Mrs. Lynne Torrey
M. Philippe Verzier
Mr. Hutton Wilkinson
Mrs. Mary Yates
M. Andrew Zega
M. Pascal Zuber

Printed in 1999
for ALAIN de GOURCUFF ÉDITEUR

Designed by Maxence Scherf
Phototypeset, photogravure, and printing by
Imprimerie Escourbiac, Graulhet (Tarn), France

Cover illustration:
View of the Orangery at Versailles during the reign of Louis XIV
Etienne Allegrain (1644-1736)
Château de Versailles. Photograph: RMN, D. Arnaudet/G.B.